NEW WATER ANTHROPOLOGY

CURATED BY GIANANDREA BARRECA

DA::Domus Academy

Coordination
Domus Academy Master in Urban Vision and Architectural Design

Curated by
Gianandrea Barreca

Projects by the students
of the Domus Academy Master
in Urban Vision and Architectural Design
2008/2012
**Charbel Attieh,
Frances Nkese Bassey,
Sonal Goyal,
Fatma Betül Karakaya,
Jin Young Kim,
Karl Maisinger,
Hideaki Nishimura,
Alia Omari,
Chien-Sheng Pan,
Melike Temiz,
Seyma Uckardesler,
Sean Yam**

Contributors
**Gianandrea Barreca,
Davide Bertin,
Andrea Bortolotti,
Matilde Cassani,
Pietro Lembi,
Francesco Librizzi,
Marco Mancini,
Alessandro Mason,
Maria Chiara Pastore,
Andrea Vercellotti,
Paola Viganò,
Sean Yam,
Federico Zanfi**

to Fabiola, Tito, Luca

INTRODUCTION

6 **Introduction**
G. Barreca

10 **Water as a regenerating element for complex urban systems**
G. Barreca

STRATEGY

30 **Porous City**
P. Viganò

36 **Between Policies and Urban Perception:
A Manifesto for the Milanese Water Systems**
S. Yam

46 **Vast territories, minute gestures:
planning commencing with water**
P. Lembi

CONNECTION

60 **Water Connections/Urban veins**
M. C. Pastore

68 **Fluid systems for urban connections**
G. Barreca

ENTERTAINMENT

78 **Aesthetics water**
F. Librizzi

90 **Water
A process of cultural sedimentation**
D. Bertin, A. Mason

THERAPY

98 **Open spaces and the water cycle
in the scattered urbanization of piedmont Lombardy.
A natural infrastructure project for Central Brianza**
F. Zanfi, A. Bortolotti

108 **Lambro System:
Recovering the water infrastructure**
A. Vercellotti

122 **Urban growth in the river valley:
the Italian experience and the doctor analogy**
M. Mancini

BUILDING

136 **Common space:
Crossovers and hybridisations between architecture and water**
G. Barreca

148 **Martesana Canal:
New ways of living along the water. Water as architecture**
M. Cassani

INTRODUCTION

Introduction

This book brings together a series of work developed over a period of time between 2008 and 2012, within the Master of Urban Vision and Architectural Design, at the Domus Academy in Milan, Italy.
Over this period, we were given the opportunity to develop, together with students and lecturers from the various programmes, research and projects related to water within complex urban contexts.
By taking a fairly limited field of action as a starting point, corresponding with the metropolitan area of Milan, we have, I think, been able to trace potential rethinking and development trajectories on the relationship between water and built up city areas. Imagining Milan as an open air laboratory, mainly through its complex, fascinating and often difficult, relationship with this precious element of urban structure design and qualification of its space, we developed ideas and specific projects which concurrently aspired to raising awareness and constructing a broader and general dimension around water in urban spaces.
That said, the idea for this book was in any case inspired by two different requirements and aspirations. Firstly, the desire to collect and acknowledge the research and project work carried out within the Master's programme. Secondly, to try to bring together the spurious and various experience developed over the course of these years, rearranging the same into one piece of work, which albeit unfinished and open, strives to outline a potential programme of intervention and development of this resource in its relationship with the constructed environments of our cities.
Finally, the book clearly bears witness to how a multiplicity of professionals and researchers, have produced reflections on this issue over time through professional work or academic research, even outside the context of this specific research.
New Water Antropology is therefore a container of a multitude of experience and personal trajectories. It is also an attempt to bring all of this together, as proof of the importance and value that this theme holds in the debate on the future identity of and public spaces in cities, especially Milan.
I certainly do not believe that this multifaceted collection of texts and images forms a programme of points which can be implemented in full, but it certainly hints at an imaginary map of actions or at least of possible desires.
In particular, the suggestions that can be drawn from cross-reading the contributions of the authors of the texts and from the design proposals developed by the students, describe a city which, by intervening in certain precise areas and through specific actions, could trigger a capillary and widespread system of interventions able to positively and favourably re-establish an ancient relationship of symbiosis between water and collective spaces, between water and architecture, and ultimately, between water and citizens.

Although its title may suggest otherwise, New Water Anthropology is not a text on anthropology or biology. Indeed, anthropology focuses its interest and attention on humans and biology should focus on water. Nevertheless, these two intimately related disciplines include certain areas that in some way intrigued me during the development of the projects and research, evolving into the common denominator of the contributions to this collection during its composition. In particular, issues relating to the theme of evolution and that of ecology especially interested me. In fact, in biology the term "evolution" is the progressive and continuous accumulation of successive changes, until manifesting, in a sufficiently broad period of time, significant morphological, structural and functional changes...". With reference to this same subject matter in another disciplinary framework, namely architecture, it can be stated that present and future history are closely connected. Furthermore, in order to reflect on the future of relationships among man, water and architecture in constructed and anthropical contexts, themes relating to the evolutionary process of these same environments have to be analysed.

The rules governing growth and contributing to forming the current "genetic heritage", the "genetic drift" resulting from the dominance of vehicles and the pursuit of maximum profit, as well as the theme of "natural selection", namely the consequent loss of parts of cities and with them certain characteristics on which the structure of the same cities was previously founded, constitute the intertwining themes in the following texts. I am particularly interested in the meaning of the term "evolution", which is often associated in many disciplines with "progress". However, the most fascinating nuance of this term lies in actual fact in its definition as "ability to change", of adaptation to the habitat in which it is located. In our relationship with water, in the constructed spaces in our cities, we have made tremendous progress, we have become "highly evolved". But, perhaps our evolution has been towards the ever greater simplification of our relationship with water. Water has disappeared from around us, while we need only to open a tap to quickly and immediately obtain it. We have become "specialised" and have lost certain characteristics and features of life, adapting to the services of a complex machine consisting of our cities. In a "parasitic" sense, we now depend on a huge collection of systems, which are often hidden and which regulate, transport, contain and control water.

Water scape, water therapy, water building constitute points and strategies for intervention in our cities, while also forming open containers for thoughts and ideas, projects and insights relating to the nature and future of relationships among water, urban spaces and citizens. These containers, the chapters subdividing the book, are the recording of a new sensitivity in the design and sharing of transformation spaces in cities, able to intimately connect the symbolic values and practical actions, the basis for creating a city's identity. A new anthropology of water means placing the innovated propensity of citizens to interact with natural elements, even and above all in constructed urban spaces, at the centre of the debate. Especially when these elements are abused and forgotten and may, if intercepted with modern and effective projects, give shape to new needs of sharing and quality of public areas in the city. It may be time to review our position as regards the relationship of water within the constructed spaces of our cities, before an extremely rapid change of conditions is able to cause excessively specialised urban systems to plummet into crisis, as with specialised forms of life.

Img. 1 - Map realized by Francesca Vargiu and Mario Abruzzese - MAPDE EXPO 2010-2011

Water as a regenerating element for complex urban systems

Water has often defined the layout and structure of cities and their architecture. In conjunction with orography, which is often a result of its action, water has produced cities that for a long time developed with it symbiotically. Over time, scientific techniques and progress have introduced new systems to control, conserve and use water. By distancing ourselves from its original character, we have violated some of its behavioural patterns and we have lost landscapes and urban spaces that in water and with water find their raison d'etre. That is, we have created of our own accord, the right conditions for uncontrollable disastrous events, which have made us realise that our cities are vulnerable and fragile in a way that we had not understood previously. Even Milan, despite its structure and "horizontal dimension" is not entirely protected from these events. However, contrary to other cities, which in the past have often had to defend themselves from water, Milan boasts a history in which water provided part of its wealth, culture and its current urban layout, which follows the outlines that with time have become sources of inspiration for the design and planning of the city's expansion. Attempts have often been made to define and describe Milan as a city of water, to explain how previously it obtained part of its wealth, culture and its current urban layout, which follows the outlines that with time have become sources of inspiration for the design and planning of the city's expansion. Milan's origins are linked to water. In fact, its historical name, Mediolanum, highlights the condition of the Terra di Mezzo, meaning a city born at the centre of a vast area, one that would soon become its most important province. Set between river couples, Ticino and Adda, Olona and Lambro, Seveso and Nirone. Since ancient times, beginning with the Gallo-Roman city, Milan has had a close relationship with water. It is positioned along the line of springs that would later give its citizens, first in the convents and then more widely, the opportunity to develop the "water-meadow" method of irrigation. Developed over 800 years ago, it was the first sign of a continuous, sustained and persistent desire to see the landscape as a project, to be moulded according to the needs of a society that for a long time had founded its wealth on agriculture (*Imgs. 1/2*). The groundwater, of which Milan has plenty, flows throughout the year at a constant temperature and is brought to the surface and left to flow across cultivated fields through a technique of engineering gentle slopes, which prevents the fields from freezing during winter and becoming too dry during summer, thereby ensuring up to eight harvests of fodder per year (*Img. 3*). That said, the intrinsic connection the city has had with water since its inception is clear, but the historically schizophrenic nature of this relationship is equally evident. On the one hand, some large Milanese rivers (Lambro, Seveso and Olona), which flow parallel from North to South, have not had any influence on the layout of the city. Milan's radial, perfect, particular shape that is built on the ruins of the Roman city, is indifferent to the rivers' course. And yet these rivers are protagonists in the wider landscape; they are the symbols around which the flourishing industrialisation of the area around northern Milan and the rich agriculture of the southern areas are set. However, it is not natural water that is at the centre of the city's urban design, but a constant and pervasive project of engineering that constructed canals, sluices, docks, basins and even ports, inspiring and supporting the radial layout of the city at the centre of the natural context given to it by the Padana plains. In Milan water has always been the result of a plan, a project and a calculation. It has accompanied the city's periods of commercial and industrial growth and even though in the 20th century it gave way to more efficient networks, which also follow the radial layout, it is still able to relate to the city. Over time, the urban space evolved and from a city of water it became a city of machines, responding to the impulses of modernity and swiftly adopting advances in technology. Already from the second half of the 19th century, with the abandonment of the waterways as the main transport network, the city, which was being influenced by the artistic avant-guard and in particular by the futurist movement that projected onto canvas and moulded with metal, shapes and images of a moving city, adapting itself to the new use of modernity with incredible speed. Without worrying about losing fragments and stories from its past and instead substituting them with new ones, the city changed its skin and transformed itself to win a place in the world. However, today the city no longer seems able to cope as rapidly with the issues, the phases of renewal and the processes of modernisation that affect the complex European urban systems with which Milan compares itself. If it is true that Milan is a city of water, it is equally true that this important element is invisible, buried, in other words, hidden from view and indifferent to the public life of the city and its citizens (*Img. 4*). Seminars to discuss the use and intrinsic value of water, planning exercises related to water or the recovery and conservation of the precious liquid and educational touring exhibitions stimulate lively debates on how to re-invent and rebuild, between the past, present and future, the relationships between water and public space and between water and citizens within our cities. In particular, it seems reasonable to say that planning and research issues related to water have until now been treated as restricted areas, attributed and connected to only one discipline and to a specific and limited location. Instead it is necessary to undertake a project that looks at the city as a whole, which standardises the individual and isolated projects and applies them to the whole city, devising a manifesto from which a governing and planning programme for water can be formulated and applied to the city and its wider surroundings, before building a list of actions. Thinking about Milan, it therefore seems necessary to develop a new anthropology of water, through a careful combination of projects and actions that consider the complexity of water's characteristics.

A manifesto that is still open that can collect different ideas, disciplines and knowledge, composite and complex research groups that are able to approach the subject from different angles; a manifesto that, through water, brings about a regeneration of the urban space simultaneously directed towards a historical, technical and aesthetic re-writing, of an important social condenser that is and must return to being public space. A document, a Water Plan that can before defining rules, gather different ideas, disciplines and knowledge, composite and complex research groups that are able to approach the subject from different angles . Other European cities with which Milan competes and compares itself have for a long time understood the value of water, not only as a resource to be preserved, but also as an element for the improvement and management of public spaces. London with the project to manage the waters of the Thames, or before that Paris with various projects from the Grand Paris programme or in Freiburg where water is fully integrated into the wider cycle of environmental sustainability. On different scales and with varying objectives, these intervention projects and programmes are living and active evidence of the interest that water commands in defining the structure, quality and competitiveness of modern European cities. A modern planning instrument cannot therefore leave out the obligation to decipher and structure this resource in its interaction with the layout of the city, with the urban space and with its inhabitants. Drawing the urban map of water, defining a role for water in the active infrastructure of the urban landscape, re-writing a new dimension for urban standards through water, affecting consumption through new building regulation parameters, connecting water and greenery within the plan for green areas, and finally giving it the modern role of an element that is able to revitalise the aesthetic codes of public space; these measures would constitute a coordinated and structured programme for the reassessment of an important element of quality and structure for the history and certainly for the future of Milan. In the following, with the intention of giving shape to this collection of aims and to open and introduce the discussions that succeed each other in the different chapters into which the book is structured, I have tried to set out some of the reasons why a strategic intervention plan for water should be prepared. At the same time I have attempted, refining the work developed with students and teachers in recent years, to indicate some interventions, some projects and some attitudes that could be put into place to varying degrees and in different contexts to put water in the spotlight and give new dignity to the relationship that it has and can again establish with the built-up areas of the city and its inhabitants.

1. Maps
Drawing the urban map of water

Throughout history, maps have represented and set on paper the image of a place at a specific time. They have been used as instruments for knowledge and work and over time they have multiplied, often incorporating an ever increasing amount of

information into their drawings. Above all, they have become more specialised, inevitably becoming more rigid and often losing their imaginative dimension and their ability to represent the entirety of a place rather than just a specific part of it.
To describe our cities we generally use maps that indicate the density of buildings, population density, municipal services, public transport or green areas. They are almost always quantitative and almost never qualitative and provide a static representation of a situation at a time and place. Maps, even contemporary and interactive ones that are able to register changes in real time, represent one of the main instruments for understanding and obtaining the sense of a place. They are therefore essential instruments onto which our visions of change, transformation and therefore planning can be projected. In truth, there are many water maps, especially historical ones for Milan, which show us the vestiges of a past that no longer exists and is now perhaps irredeemably part of the lost city. In contrast, the modern ones are often very technical and intended for professional use. Networks and grids of piping and underground utilities, jumbles of lines and symbols that are often indecipherable to non-experts, an expression of the complexity that is often hidden beneath our streets and is ultimately intangible and distant from our daily lives. However, these maps are not adequate to establish a new relationship between water, public space, buildings and citizens; they are not integrated and are difficult to integrate into the design of the city and its material and immaterial flows of people and things. It is therefore necessary to completely re-think them and draw new maps. On the horizontal plane, resting on the ground, manholes, drinking fountains, etc., as well as on the vertical plane, drains, gutters, etc., are new elements to include in maps, to give us instruments to represent the fluid nature of water, that draw iridescent and changing landscapes difficult to set within a static medium. We need maps that integrate the top and the bottom, the horizontal plane and the vertical, and which contain all the elements capable of transporting, containing and releasing water in the space of the city in which we live. (*Imgs. 5/6/7/8/9/10*)

2. Methods
Water, a new dimension for urban standards

In the various methods that the municipal authorities use to regulate and plan the development of our cities, there are commercial plans, those related to traffic, as well as those for services and the urban standards for green spaces and building, and of course in some of the documents there is something regarding the supply and consumption of water. Certainly it is very difficult to find documents and more so maps and specific directions that regulate the issue of water and its relationship with the city's public space in a structured manner. For every new building or renovation project, the number of parking spaces and the number of square metres of solar panels needed, plus the square metres that will be surrendered to the town council, etc., are all established. But apart from setting a percentage of drainage area to be left free "to breathe" and the amount of water measured in litres per second that can be introduced into the communal sewers, no other specifications, neither quantitative nor, more importantly, qualitative, seem to be made in relation to water. For example, the number of square metres of water surface that should be released or introduced into a park, or how many fountains, water features or hydraulic machines that should or could be installed in town squares is not written down; neither is, more importantly, the number of square metres or litres per person that should reasonably be created in order to obtain better urban standards. (*Img. 11*) Quantity has never been necessarily synonymous with quality and the requirement of 18 square metres of green space per inhabitant has certainly not been enough to ensure the urban quality that we need. However, defining some numbers, some minimum quantities, would be a start, a point from which to experiment in the city with, for example, what effect would be achieved by providing and substituting asphalt with water. Perhaps, starting immediately, changing the horizontal skin of our cities would be sufficient, it would be enough to peel off the asphalt from some wide spaces and squares and allow the earth to breathe, absorb the rain or hold on to it where its composition permits, in this way re-designing a pavement and a luminous, softer urban dimension. (*Img. 12*)

3. Therapies
Rehabilitate, connect, integrate

Water is the source of life. Negligence, abandonment and greed in many parts of the world have meant that water has often lost that vocation. Pollution and urbanisation have wasted and sometimes destroyed the value that water carries with it. Trapped and constricted in our artificial constructions it has often rebelled, causing floods and destruction. Frequently contaminated by pollutants that it has transported rapidly and then released, spreading poison and death over vast areas. It is certainly not possible to plan a strategic general project on water, in any context or in any city, without first launching a new era of respect and recovery for the quality of already present water, both surface and subterranean. Water can cleanse contaminated ground, water can be used to activate natural filtration and purification systems, but first water must itself be purified, first the balance of the whole system must be restored. In many countries of northern Europe, projects to restore the urban sections of river courses have been made possible by means of interventions carried out starting upstream and along the entire course of the river. In relation to Milan, we can certainly talk about using water to purify abandoned industrial areas, about transforming canals that organise and structure the landscape as new tourist routes and new ecological corridors. We can also discuss the re-opening of sections of canal in the inner circle, but first of all, without any doubt, the raw material, that is water, must be restored. There is no certainty that a number of small interventions put together will produce a significant and effective outcome. One large planning and intervention project that approaches the problem with the necessary breadth would be more suitable. Perhaps that would be possible in a virgin landscape and under circumstances in which regional institutions and private individuals could and managed to coordinate themselves and work together. But the intensely urbanised structure of the territory in the Milan region and the multitude of persons who in different ways control the waters, certainly do not satisfy the conditions described previously. From the Ticino to the Adda, from the Olona to the Lambro through the Seveso, the urban stretches of these water courses should re-appropriate and in a sense widen their banks, they should take back the un-built and abandoned spaces that are present along their courses, the disused industrial areas to transform them into areas for restoring and regenerating the waters, thereby implicitly creating a natural laboratory for good purification practices along their courses (*Imgs. 13/14/15*). Lastly, integration means a departure from the approach whereby policies are often sector specific and the frequently specialist disciplines do not communicate. Once upon a time, in fact not very long ago, architecture, engineering and hydraulics cohabited in the buildings and infrastructure that gave shape to our urban landscapes and our city. There can be no future without devising a convergence of policies and projects in disciplines, which by becoming specialised have become distant and which through explaining and defining themselves autonomously have become rigid, losing the ability to have a dialogue and hybridise.

4. Rediscovery
Beginning with history to design the future

In the evolutionary history of all complex urban contexts, water has always held strategic importance. Water has often defined the shape and the structure of cities and their architecture, and has given shape and life to cities that have for a long time developed in symbiosis with them. Between history and vision, lost relationships can certainly be rediscovered; subterranean rivers and lakes, abandoned or disused quarries, canals that have long since been closed or those that are still open but are partially forgotten, they represent a chance to redeem public space and an opportunity to regenerate part of that intense and fantastic network that structured and designed the shape of the city and to reconstruct the intimate relationship between city and water that has been almost entirely lost (if discovery is the logic consequence of discovering things, countries and truths, then rediscovery simply means returning to carefully and intimately consider certain elements that have already been discovered). Rediscovering water means returning to construct a relationship, new and contemporary, with an important factor for the character, design and significance of our city, of all the cities that over time have abused, wasted and denied this ancestral need for cohabitation with and proximity to the natural elements around us. It certainly is not the cost, nor the complex network of infrastructure and underground utilities that run beneath the surface that should lead us to refuse a possible reopening of the canals or other urban hydraulic systems. Instead, what needs to be removed is the risk of starting a "romantic" style of process directed towards restoring a past that perhaps does not make sense to resurrect. Therefore, at the centre of this rediscovery should not be water infrastructure, manufactured architectural and engineering goods, old and recent, but water itself and its potential as a motor for new ecosystems, as a modern protagonist of urban regeneration, as a connecting line between seemingly distant urban systems and places, as a condenser of meanings and a vehicle for a renewed urban ecology. In Milan, Conca del Naviglio, the last stretch of the Martesana, near Via San Marco, as well as the Vettabbia stretch running from Ticinello park to the Darsena, could activate new unexpected links within the urban context, routes and ecological and environmental systems that without necessarily involving the entire old network, could represent important ways to rediscover and at the same time renovate the urban structure. (*Imgs. 16/17*)

5. Codes
For a new water aesthetic

Looking back, the relationship between human settlement and water has generated the development of architecture and urban design alongside the development of construction techniques. Fountains and water features, routes, pools and fish farms have represented and have sometimes become essential elements of public space, often able to anticipate and innovate in terms of aesthetic codes, halfway between engineering and architecture, between architecture and sculpture, between work of art and urban furnishings. Therefore, the history of these elements is very interesting, that in our cities they have experienced a continuous fluctuation between moments of success and long periods of abandonment. Today, in an urban context that needs quality, putting water at the centre could also mean inventing new guidelines for the restoration and interaction of public space and citizens who use water as a means of connection. Far from any nostalgic approach, along the circle of the Spanish walls, in the urban parks or even in the circle of the interior canals such as those that stretch into the urbanised territory of the sprawling city, within a holistic project, a series of new water guidelines, an expression of the union between history, technology and aesthetics, could have the ability to renew and experiment with new aesthetic codes and innovative relationships between the city and its water system. (*Imgs. 18/19*)
Reconnecting and condensing the three important elements that characterise and define the complex relationship between Milan and the water, that is history, technology and design, within one project in the public space of the city, and introducing certain principles and rules to govern the fluids with machines invented by Leonardo, Torricelli and Bernulli, could offer a way to reactivate the lost connection between inhabitants, architecture, urban space and water. (*Img. 20*)

6. Artefacts
Collect, contain, reverse, exhibit

Today more than ever, in order to re-establish contact with water and the natural elements, architecture needs to get involved and return to being a support, a container and a machine for water. Architecture needs to give evidence of the importance that water holds today in the "survival" of our buildings and for the functioning of our urban systems. But most of all architecture also needs to become the representation of a renewed sensitivity towards the primary elements in our surroundings. Overcoming some solutions suggested by ephemeral and temporary architecture, and turning towards the principle of architecture as a synthesis of technological efficiency, we could outline some approaches that could be used to reassess our buildings.

One approach could be that of "collecting" water. Water could be collected on roofs and façades thereby allowing our buildings to be transformed and making this new sensitivity apparent. A second approach could be to "contain" water inside our buildings, starting again to construct impluvia and tanks with the aim of creating collective spaces and healthy ecological micro-systems. A third approach could be to "reverse" the skin of the building and make visible the lymphatic system that irrigates our buildings, running throughout them. A venous architecture that brings the plumbing system that feeds every vital part of buildings to the exterior, onto its skin.

Finally, a fourth approach could be to "exhibit" water on the exterior. Many buildings that for various reasons are constructed to contain water internally are often organised according to strict rules, hidden from view and they are developed behind closed doors. Opening them up to reveal the reason for their existence could build an interesting new way to uncover the presence of water inside. It is clear that all these project dimensions and topics for research and consideration, should be pursued together; they should be part of one project and an open vision of the future for Milan and for every city that is interested in rebuilding the lost or forgotten important relationships with water. All the topics should interconnect and overlap to create one basis of reference that understands water as a possible instrument for the regeneration of our cities' space and architecture. Water as a source of energy, always renewable, able to design a new technological/natural landscape that is as urban as it is natural. This landscape should not be understood as a simple restoration of an ecosystem and original structure, now compromised and almost entirely gone, but as a suggestion and stimulus for the conception of a new system of solutions in which water may re-emerge and be used for its power and its symbolic and environmental ability (*Imgs. 21/22/23*).

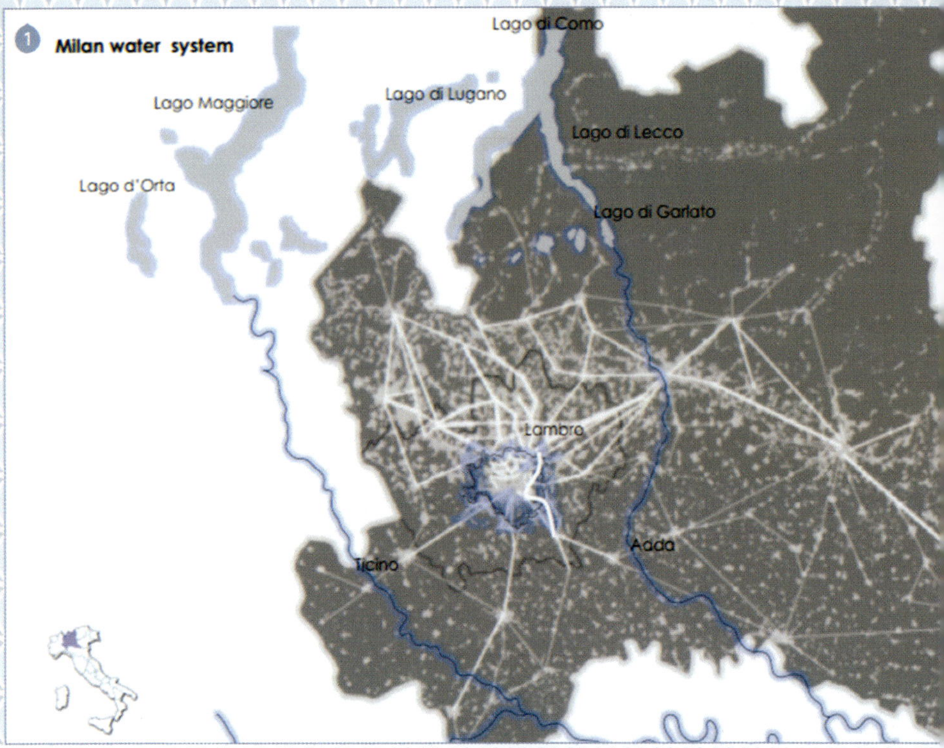

Img. 1 - Milan water system. Project title: "Remediation infrastructure" by Charbel Attieh - Final Master Project 2011.
Img. 2 - "Le marcite": cultivation technique characteristic of the Po Valley
Img. 3 - Milan water system. Project title: "Remediation infrastructure" by Charbel Attieh - Final Master Project 2011
Img. 4 - Island of Milan swimming on groundwater . Project title: "Draining city - groundwater in Milan" by Karl Maisinger Final Master Project 2010.

INTRODUCTION

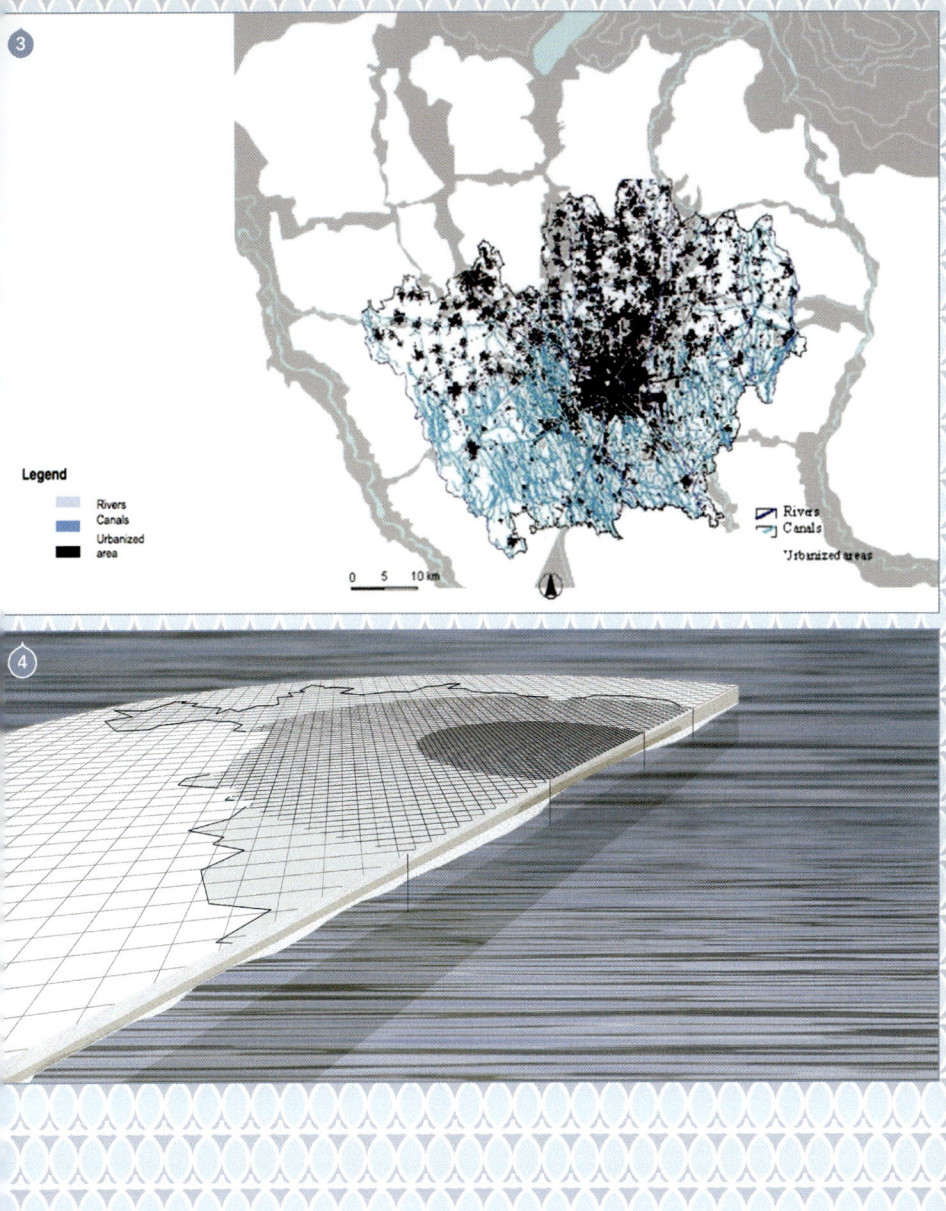

G. BARRECA 019

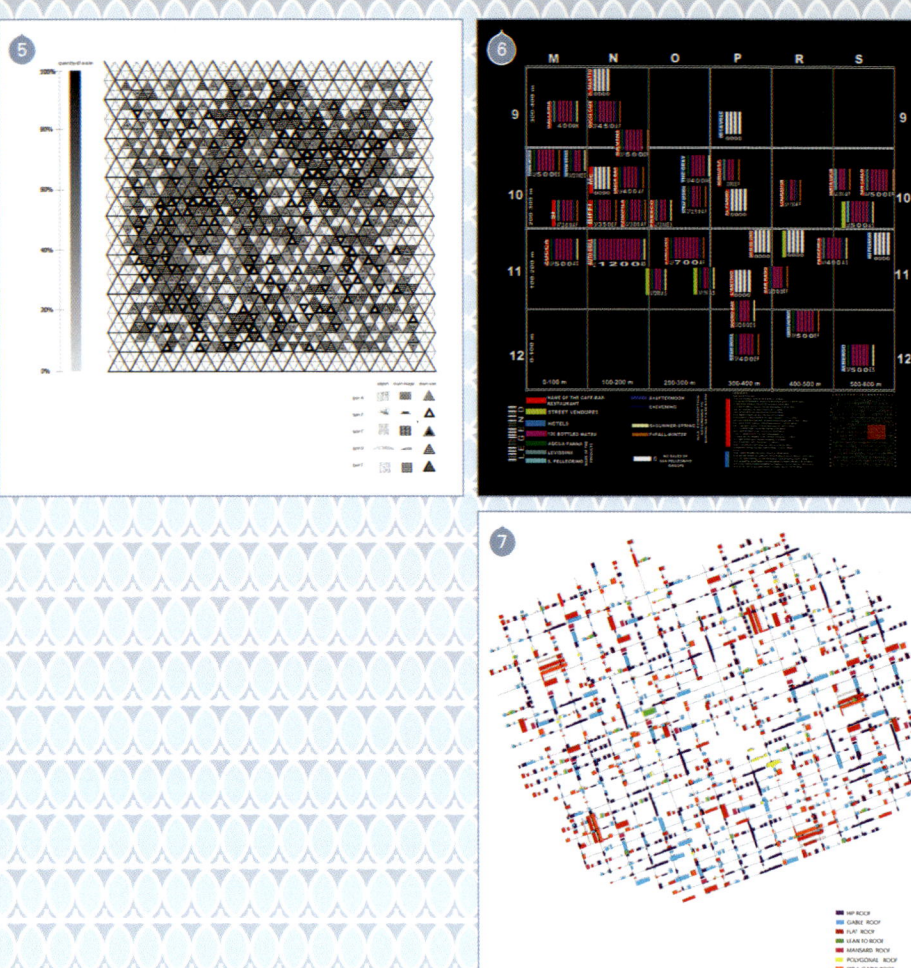

Img. 5 - Mapping Milan: Breathing Milan - The water device in the public space by Jin Young Kim
Img. 6 - Mapping Milan: Bottled water in Milan by Fatma Betül Karakaya
Img. 7 - Mapping Milan: Covering the buildings skin – The roof as a collector by Frances Nkese Bassey
Img. 8 - Mapping Milan: Urban vessel network system by Hideaki Nishimura
Img. 9 - Mapping Milan: Pool on the road by Seyma Uckardesler
Img. 10- Mapping Milan: Virtual water by Charbel Attieh

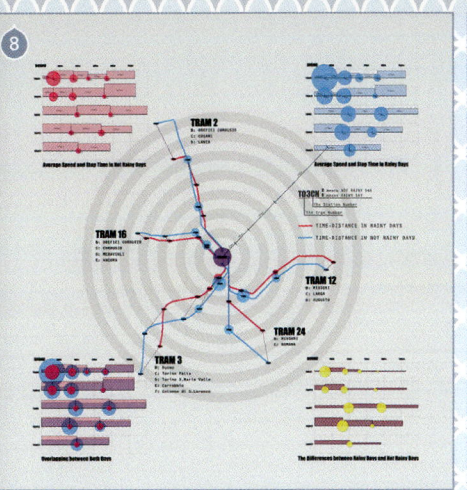
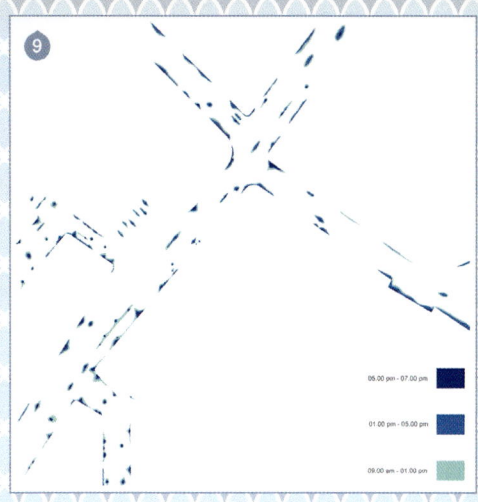
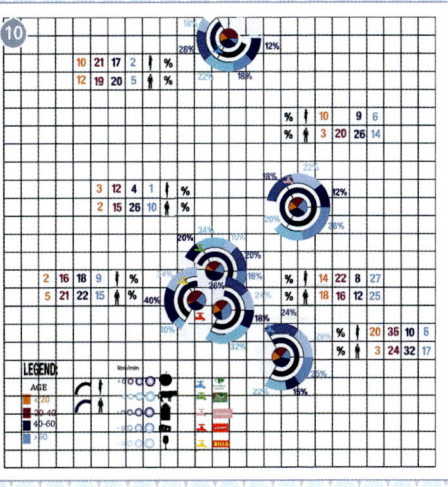

G. BARRECA

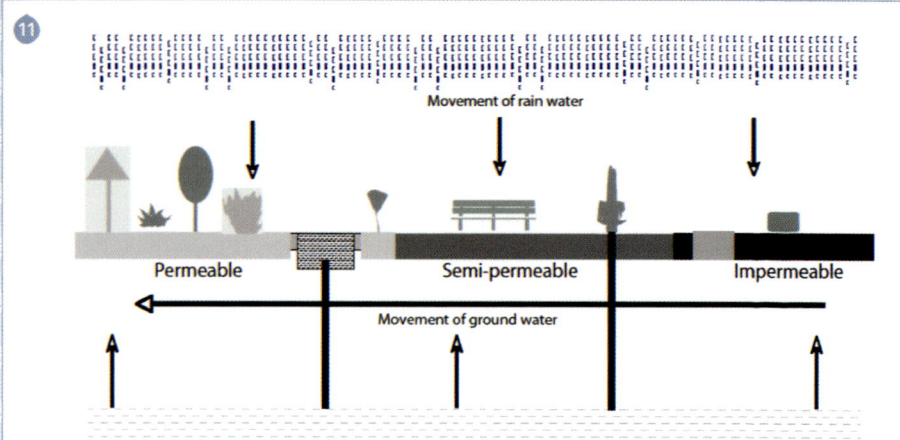

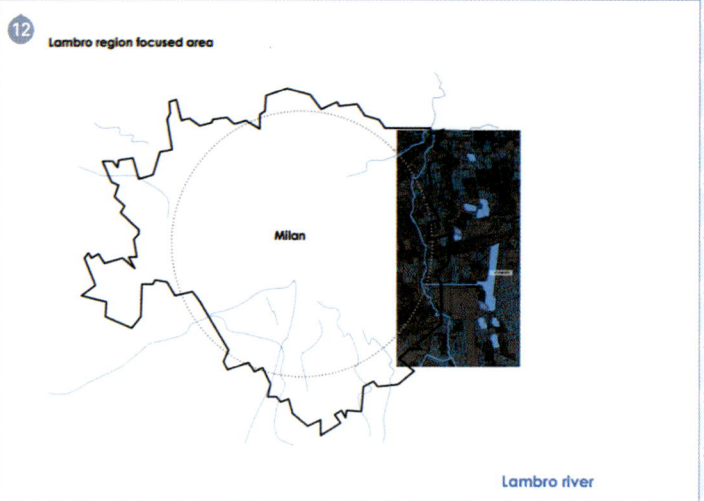

Img. 11 - Abacus for spring - wet season - rain water by Sean Yam and Sonal Goyal. Project title: "The surface is more then Deep" - Strategies and Vision for a Water City, 2011.
Img. 12 - Water purification wetland. Project title: "Remediation infrastructure" by Charbel Attieh - Final Master Project 2011
Img. 13 - Section of Wetland by Charbel Attieh, Sonal Goyal, Frances Nkese Bassey, Okpoyo. Project title: "Milan Water City - Water as element for regenerating complex urban systems, 2010-2011".
Img. 14 - Water purification wetland. Project title: "Remediation infrastructure" by Charbel Attieh - Final Master Project 2011.
Img. 15 - Water purification wetland. Project title: "Remediation infrastructure" by Charbel Attieh - Final Master Project 2011.

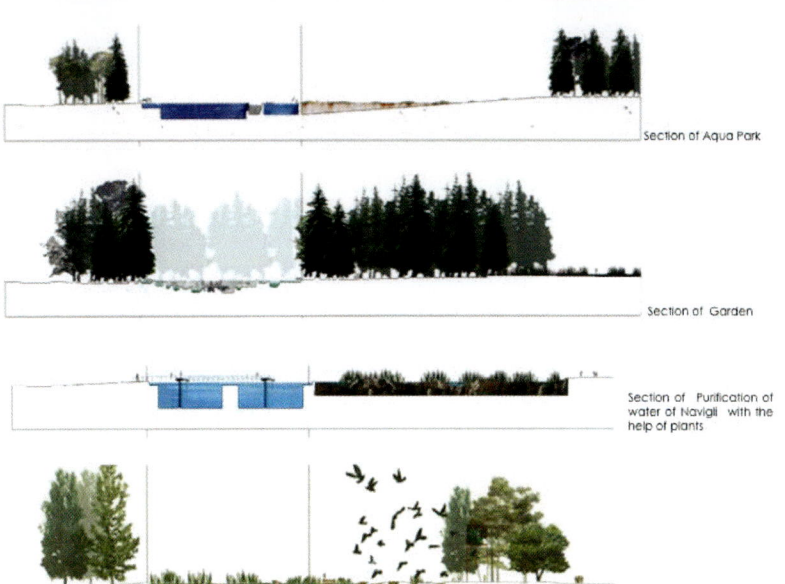

Section of Aqua Park

Section of Garden

Section of Purification of water of Navigli with the help of plants

Section of Wetland

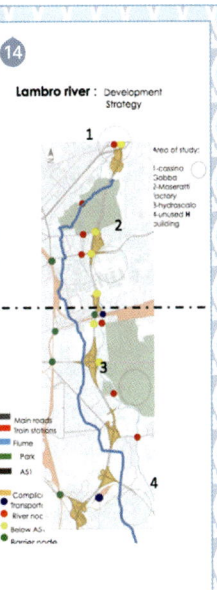

Lambro river : Development Strategy

Area of study:
1-casinò Gobba
2-Maseratti factory
3-hydroscalo
4-unused H building

Main roads
Train stations
Flume
Park
ASI
Complici transport
River noc
Below ASI
Barrier node

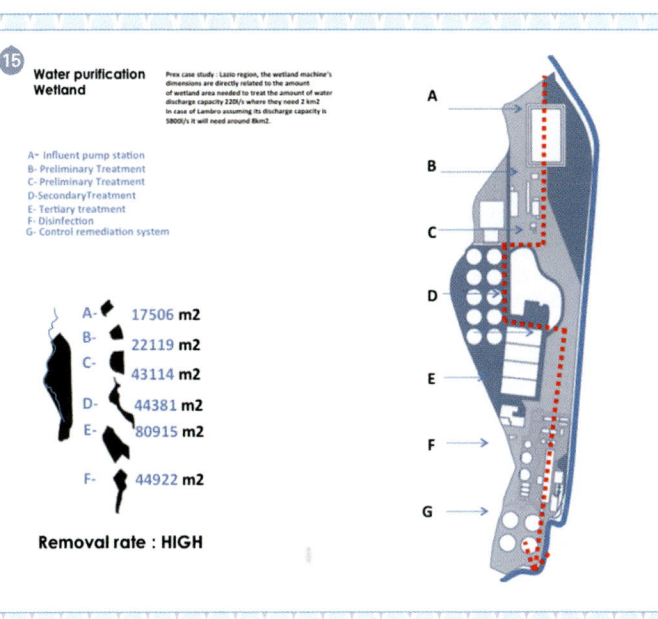

Water purification Wetland

Prea case study : Lazio region, the wetland machine's dimensions are directly related to the amount of wetland area needed to treat the amount of water discharge capacity 220l/s where they need 2 km2. In case of Lambro assuming its discharge capacity is 5800l/s it will need around 8km2.

A- Influent pump station
B- Preliminary Treatment
C- Preliminary Treatment
D- Secondary Treatment
E- Tertiary treatment
F- Disinfection
G- Control remediation system

A- 17506 m2
B- 22119 m2
C- 43114 m2
D- 44381 m2
E- 80915 m2
F- 44922 m2

Removal rate : HIGH

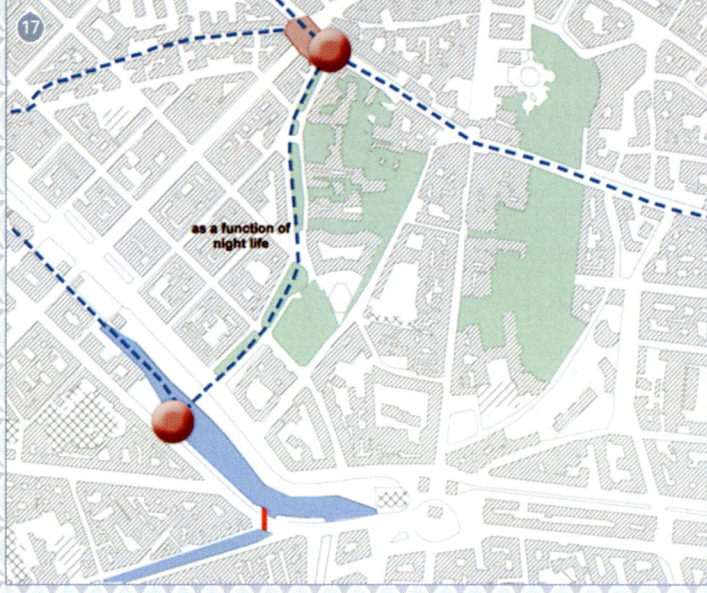

Img. 16 - The settlement system. Project title: "Rediscovering Navigli, between history and vision" by Melike Temiz - Final Master Project 2011.
Img. 17 - Portions to be re-opened. Project title: "Rediscovering Navigli, between history and vision" by Melike Temiz - Final Master Project 2011.
Img. 18 - Triadic water concerto. Project title: "Triadic water concerto" by Hideaki Nishimura - Final Master Project 2011.

G. BARRECA

Img. 19 - Promenade aqueduct fr the area Giardini Pubblici Indro Montanelli, design concept and general view.
  Image by Hideaki Nishimura from "Triadic water concerto" - Final Master Project 2011.
Img. 20 - Image by Hideaki Nishimura from "Triadic water concerto" - Final Master Project 2011.
Img. 21 - Models of the machines created: spatial signs that come to life through water and generate spatial signs
  able to create harmonious vibrations of sound, which require a "slowing down of thought" by A.Mason
Img. 22 - The vibrator- Explanation. Project: Sensitive water machine by Chien-Sheng Pan, 2011.
Img. 23 - Machine explanation. Project title: "Sensitive water machine" by Chien-Sheng Pan - Final Master Project 2011.

G. BARRECA

STRATEGY

Porous City

For some time now, I have been reflecting on the concept of porosity and how it can effectively contribute as a research and design tool for cities and territories. Observing the ability of a body to allow itself to be penetrated, the relationship between empty shapes and movement passing through them, the nexus with certain other concepts, such as those of permeability and connectivity, stimulates a deep-rooted integration between ecological rationality and city design.

The land housing water and how this is viewed has in recent years provided important opportunities to reconsider design on different scales: the reconstitution of porous and permeable spaces, the reconnection of interrupted, hidden, diverted or fragmented water systems, the slowing down of channelled and excessively fast water flows, the extension of space for water in order to reduce ever increasing risks, constitute occasions to re-read the territory's shape and to design the same. Water, in its complex rationality, changes, draws, designs cities. Water as an agent reintroduces to architecture and urban planning focus on territorial support, on time and transience, and on biotic relations. It is the modifying action of water and not only the design of water that needs to be integrated in every design featuring the same. It is because water is an agent of transformation that its dynamics need to be fully understood, in order to prevent it from acting against any formal attempt of reduction.

The porous city can be understood in sections: when we think of skin pores, we are unable to imagine the process of substance absorption by merely observing the surface. The different layers of the city's porous skin needs to be understood in detail by observing its depressions, cavities, the type of ground and its capacity to retain water or, conversely, to enable it to penetrate. A lot is required of this surface: to absorb, to allow to breathe, to define public space. Commencing from the theme of water, even often abstract reflections on the sharing of the spaces become real. Water designs and its design may become a tool to redefine cities and to support the same.

In certain research and design experiences, the need to reduce CO_2 emissions, increasing water-related risks, in addition to changes in irrigation techniques, have enabled us to delineate even radical scenarios to reinterpret and re-use water infrastructures, consequently providing opportunities to construct public spaces on a territorial scale.

030 STRATEGY

1. Networks

Road and water networks in the extensive Venetian city appear to be the result of innumerable attempts to introduce forms of rationality over long periods of time and over extended spaces. This is a fixed social capital, an "immense repository of effort" made of roads, water courses, irrigation and drainage networks, which now await to be rethought under different conditions to those of the past[1].

In the plains of the Veneto region, traversed by an extremely dense irrigation network (in the dry high plains) and a drainage network (in the moist lowlands where the slopes, in addition to the impervious soil, makes water drainage difficult), water is both a scarce resource that needs to be retained and an element producing insecurity and extended risks which needs to be expelled. Reusing the disused gravel pits of the high plain, connecting them to the rivers through the network of channels to reduce flooding, enhancing the lower water grid in the lowlands to slow down and store water: these actions may not only resolve some of the current problems relating to widespread settlements in the territories, but also enrich them with a network of multi-functional spaces. The maintenance of reclamation areas, or areas below or at sea level, along the edge of the lagoon, which are subjected to climate stresses destined to increase over time and which have high energy costs, may need to be rethought. The selection of areas (settlements and landscapes) to be protected against rising sea levels and areas in which water is to be reintroduced, the introduction of types of farming suitable to new conditions will lead to the design new geographies.

---

1. Viganò P., 2008, "Water and Asphalt, The Project of Isotropy in the Metropolitan Region of Venice", Architectural Design, vol. 78; Viganò P., U. Degli Uberti, G. Lambrecht, T. Lombardo, G. Zaccariotto., 2009, Landscapes of water. Paesaggi dell'acqua, Pordenone: Risma Editrice; Fabian, L., Viganò, P., eds., 2010, Extreme City - Climate Change and the transformation of the waterscape, Università IUAV di Venezia; Viganò P., 2011, "The project of isotropy", in Ferrario V., Sampieri A., Viganò P., eds., Landscapes of Urbanism, Q5,Officina, Rome.

P. VIGANÒ

2. Porous city

During the study on the Grand Paris and on a number of occasions over subsequent years when flood risks in the southern areas of Paris were discussed[2], one of the strategies of the ville poreuse project focused on water space. The lack of perception of the risks that Paris is subjected to is in itself a problem, despite the detailed descriptions of noirs such as Crimes de Seine[3], which unwind along with the gradual rise of water from the innumerable cavities of the metropolis. Minimising the considerable water risks, which will worsen with climate change upstream from Paris in the Seine valley, implies that the areas which can be conceived as resilient (the changing areas in which projects can be transformed into water storage spaces) and areas which, on the other hand, should be protected using all known defence techniques (embankments, walls, provisional protection systems...) need to be clarified. This requires that the relationship between the centre and suburbs (the area of the Seine en Amont has always been conceived as a "servant" of the metropolis), in addition to the definition of habitable land, be reconsidered. If in the past, industries, places of energy production and waste disposal unravelled along the Siene,... today new parts of the city are being built, while existing centres become more and more dense, increasing the risks that the territory is subjected to. But the mere settlement of a population is not sufficient to define the habitability of a place. This is to be defined by taking risks into account: in allowing accessibility even during flooding, in protecting areas that cannot and will not be subjected to major renovations such as those that will take place in certain areas. Even in this case, the geography of waters and the risks related to the same introduce political and ecological issues full of controversies and contradictions. The relationship between design and ecological rationality, legitimately present in discussions with other forms of rationality which traditionally direct the transformation cities, is one of the most interesting aspects of current research[4]. Water is not only an essential element of urban functioning, but also a rationality causing it to change. We need to collectively understand how the different forms of rationality can establish a dialogue within forms of social organisation and spaces which differ to those from the past and which are subjected to new demands.

Reflections which commence with water, from its grammar and syntax, may be among the guiding elements of a design able to intersect many of the practices of contemporary territories: an integrated, multifunctional and multi-scale design that requires new alliances and allows for metropolitan and territorial spaces to be appropriated. New themes through city design.

2. Secchi, B., Viganò, P., La ville poreuse – Un projet pour le Grand Paris et la métropole de l'après-Kyoto, Metis-Presses, Genève, 2011; Studio 012 Bernardo Secchi, Paola Viganò, Roberto Sega, Ilaria Mancini, Laure Thierrée, con Mageo, Biodiversita, Seine Amont Elaboration d'une schéma de cohérence paysagère et urbaine de la Vallée de la Seine en amont. EPA Orsa, March 2012.
3. Danielle Thiéry, 2011, Crimes de Seine, Payot &Rivage.
4. Viganò P., 2013, "Urbanism and Ecological Rationality", in Pickett, S.T.A.; Cadenasso, M.L.; McGrath, Brian eds., Resilience in Ecology and Urban Design, Springer.

STRATEGY

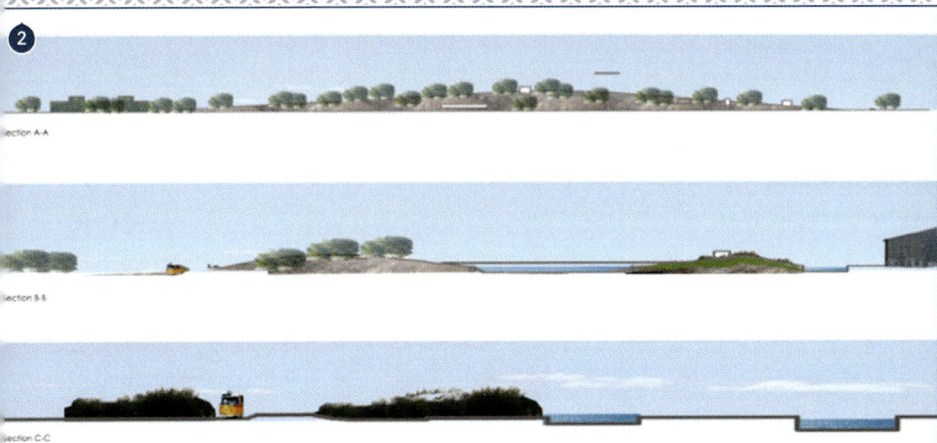

Img. 1 - Scenario. Project title: Landscape sinfonia by Hideaki Nishimura, Chien-Sheng Pan and Jin Young Kim Workshop: Liquid Patterns, 2011

Img. 2 - Sections. Project title: Landscape sinfonia by Hideaki Nishimura, Chien-Sheng Pan, Sonal Goyal and Jin Young Kim Workshop: Liquid Patterns, 2011.

3

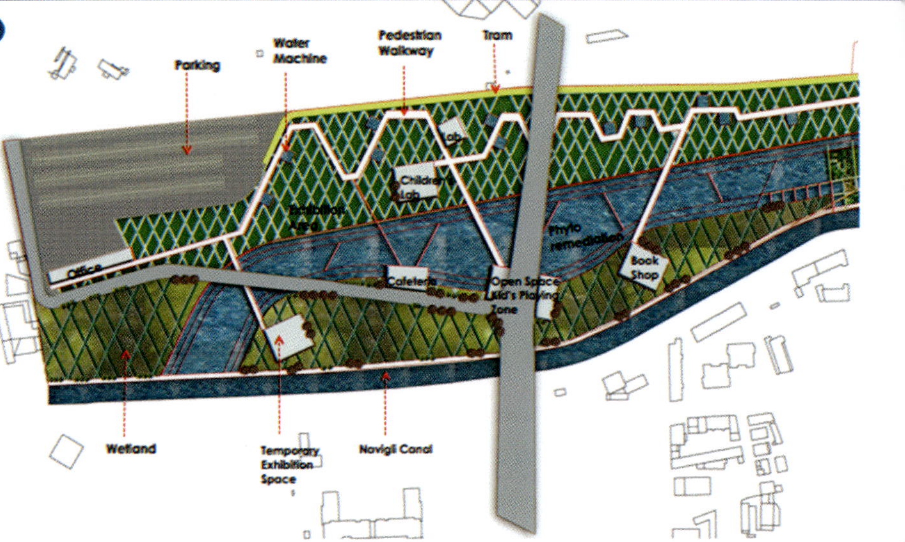
Parking
Water Machine
Pedestrian Walkway
Tram
Lab
Children's Lab
Exhibition Area
Phyto remediation
Office
Cafeteria
Open Space Kid's Playing Zone
Book Shop
Wetland
Temporary Exhibition Space
Navigli Canal

4

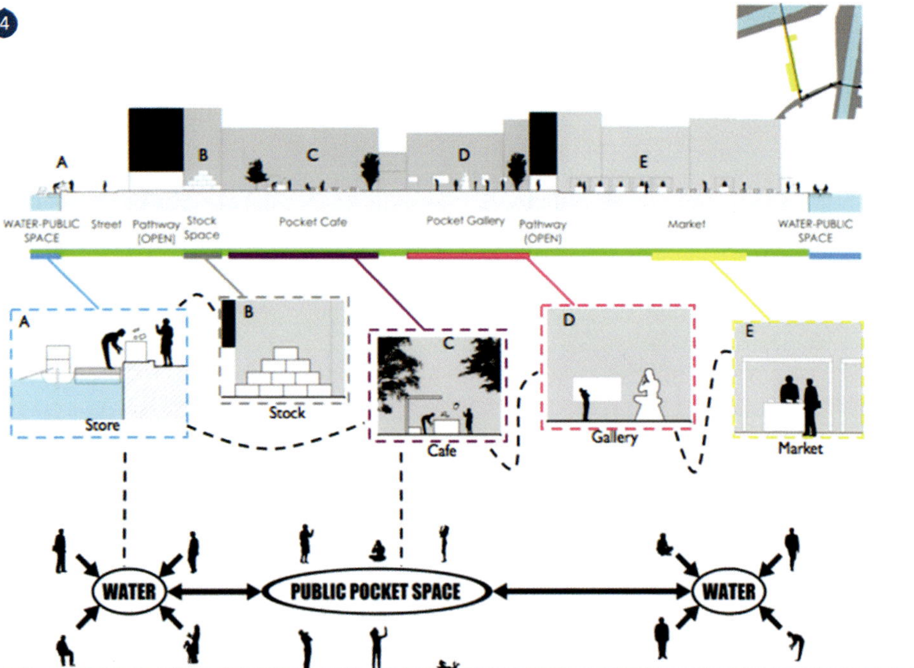
A
B
C
D
E
WATER-PUBLIC SPACE
Street
Pathway (OPEN)
Stock Space
Pocket Cafe
Pocket Gallery
Pathway (OPEN)
Market
WATER-PUBLIC SPACE
Store
Stock
Cafe
Gallery
Market
WATER
PUBLIC POCKET SPACE
WATER

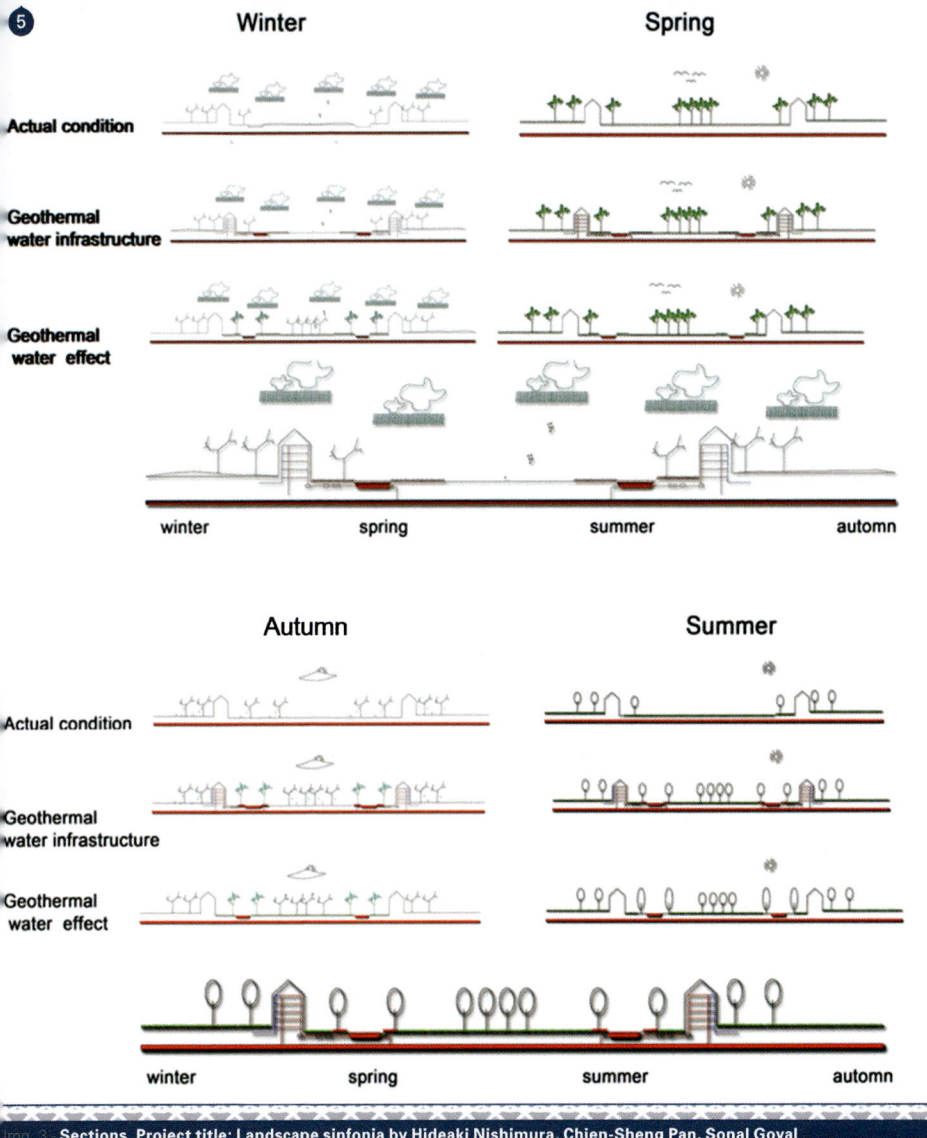

Img. 3 - Sections. Project title: Landscape sinfonia by Hideaki Nishimura, Chien-Sheng Pan, Sonal Goyal and Jim Young Kim Workshop: Liquid Patterns, 2011.
Img. 4 - New connections. Project title: Energy flow city by Hideaki Nishimura and Chien-Sheng Pan. Workshop: Strategies and Visions for a Water City, 2011.
Img. 5 - Wetland during seasons. Project title: Parco Solari by Alia Omari, Charbel Attieh - 2011.

Between Policies and Urban Perception:
A Manifesto for the Milanese Water Systems

This short paper proposes a new framework for understanding and managing the diverse water systems in the metropolitan Milanese territory[5] in the form of a strategic manifesto consisting of twenty-four policy statements grouped into five themes. At its core, I postulate that Milan's future wellbeing is contingent on the city's civic and political reengagement with water. From the great lakes of Italy directly north of the city to the rivers and streams that flow around Milan on the Po Plain to the city's thousand-year-old history of water infrastructure, Milan's relationship with water is ancient, rich, and inescapable. In an age where words such as 'sustainability,' 'greening,' and 'ecology' have become central to political, commercial, and public discourse, Milan's role as one of the world's primary centres of international design, architecture, and fashion cannot be sustained if the city's chronic urban planning problems of excessive water consumption and lack of visible and meaningful public green space and water infrastructures are not resolved (*Img. 1*). Indeed, without greater consciousness about water vis-à-vis the city, the daily lives of the Milanese and the experiences of visitors will be diminished. Water can and must be the principal tool the city employs to address its most pressing urban design challenges. In essence, water is Milan's 'only way out.' Without water, the city cannot solve the abovementioned problems. By examining the main themes[6] of water aesthetics, water consumption, water infrastructure, water in the history and memory of the city, water and the permeability of the city, and water in mapping the city, I propose to develop a framework to begin the process of reclaiming the city's lost relationship with water. The genesis of the thesis on which this paper is based is the body of work developed by the 2011 class of the Masters in Urban Vision and Architectural Design (MUVAD) program of the Domus Academy in Milan, for which the unifying theme through five workshops was water. The six topical chapters of my original thesis were reached through a process of 'mind mapping' (*Img. 2*). First, a list of all pertinent projects and lectures from the year was compiled and then connected to the major course topics and titles as written in the five workshop briefs that comprised the first two trimesters of the year. From here, the 'master list' of topics was annotated with key words that I believe best describe the category(ies) under which a subject fits. From this analysis, the most prevalent key words were counted, measured against one another, and finally re-worded to form the six chapters. The final distillation of my research results in a "water policy manifesto" for the Milanese metropolis consisting of twenty-four points organized into five new "action areas" below.

5. This short chapter is largely based on my Master's thesis and represents a greatly edited and truncated version of that text. Sean Frederic Yam, [Masters Thesis], Still Waters Run Deep: A Manifesto for the Water Systems of the Milanese Metropolis, Milano: MUVAD, Department of Urban and Landscape Design, Domus Academy, 2011.

6. These six themes form the primary topical chapters of my Master's thesis.

STRATEGY

1. Governance

- Because it is a public asset, any future policies or practices impacting public access to the Milanese water system must be developed via an open and fully participatory process (e.g., referenda, citizen engagement initiatives, et cetera).
- Self-sufficiency, ecological responsibility, and civic engagement are the overarching principles under which any new water infrastructures are developed.
- The recovery and improvement of the city's historic relationship with water is contingent on collaborative dialogue and action amongst all relevant actors that transcend jurisdictional, territorial and sectoral boundaries.
- Given that the Comune di Milano is part of a much larger hydrological system, policies and programs affecting and addressing the city's horizontal and vertical layers can only be successful if developed and implemented on an intergovernmental basis (involving other municipalities, provinces, and the Region of Lombardy). Water is a fundamental public good and water consumption a fundamental social, political and ecological issue. Water, then, must serve a human-hearted and not blindly commercial agenda.

2. Awareness and branding

- To reduce wasteful consumption, social awareness and educational initiatives must be developed. Research into promising practices illustrates that the money spent on preventative societal education is as important as and is better value than interventional projects.
- Educational programs should focus on celebrating the high quality of drinking water in Milan, the need to maintain this quality and to prevent/reduce water pollution, reasons to drink low-cost but high-quality public tap water, and the need to reduce wasteful domestic water use.
- The city's water bodies and systems form a critical component of Milan's "brand," and future marketing and educational campaigns highlight the unique characteristics of the Milanese water systems (e.g., the ancient network of freshwater canals and the vast "seas" of underground freshwater in the metropolitan area).
- A new collective memory must be crafted where knowledge about and concern for water is a prominent factor of the Milanese identity.
- The process of mapping, the knowledge revealed through mapping, and the visual representation of data in maps, are powerful tools that can educate the public about the importance of urban water issues.

3. Public space for social functions
- Water aesthetics foster leisure and educational opportunities for citizens.
- Through the aesthetics of water, a balance and harmony can be negotiated between spaces for public social functions and those for private contemplation in the city (*Img. 3*).
- As water traverses all scales, projects for the "skin" of the metropolis must also be undertaken on an inter-scalar basis with a goal of creating better public space on all scales – from the neighbourhood garden to the regional nature reserve.

4. Responsible ecology
- True urban autonomy should lead to the creation of an "off-grid city" where self-sufficient but politically and socially engaged units of individuals and communities comprise a city.
- Precious urban voids are transformed into functional and useful "landscapes of necessity" for purposes such as energy production and excess heat and carbon emissions reduction.
- Water and greenery work symbiotically to create "living landscapes of decontamination" where plant life remediates polluted land, air, and water, and these elements in turn nurture the plants that clean them.
- Successful interventions to improve the skin of the city must take into account all surface types as well as all water types (rain, groundwater, etc.), and understand that the skin and water of the city function as a single interdependent system that is not only horizontal but highly vertical as well. That is, the city's visible skin is merely the ultimate layer in a highly stratified subterranean subsystem of interacting solid and liquid layers (*Img. 4*).
- By designing with water and with the city's skin, responsible strategies can improve the life of the city in terms of flood remediation, protecting living "green" surfaces, and reducing water and energy consumption.

5. Design theories for the future city
- Water mediates the disparate elements that comprise the contemporary cityscape.
- A new monumentality of water aesthetics serves a democratic calling and is both ephemeral and portable in its design.
- History and water work in tandem to redesign the city. Water elements are a reminder of the rich history of the city and historical elements are a reminder of the city's ancient and inexorable relationship with water. This relationship, however, is not wedded to the past. Rather, it forms the epistemological foundation on which water and the constructed city come together to create improved civic assets (*Img .5*).
- Water maps that bring to light new information as well as those that uncover long lost urban connections inspire interventions that better connect water, citizens, and the city.

- New maps exploring water expose the countless and vital ways in which water and the city are indelibly networked, and in doing so, underline the need to consider water as a fundamental element of designing Milan's future.
- Mapping is an inter-scalar process and water is an inter-scalar element. Together, mapping with water reinforces the need to plan and manage the city's hydrological systems on a cohesive inter-scalar basis.

Reading the final manifesto, several new thematic "currents" emerged that define this body of text. The twenty-four points that comprise the manifesto have thus been organized under five new categories that I found particularly resonant. Each category is named and arranged in such a way as to allow a reader to use the manifesto (either as an extant document or broken down into its constituent points and themes) as an intellectual framework or policy plan with which to create more detailed and focused interventions to improve the state of Milan vis-à-vis its water systems. "Governance" speaks broadly to the need for civil society to engage with water issues. "Awareness and Branding" stems from a strong trend in my research illustrating that social concern is critical to change and that educating the citizenry and raising awareness is a crucial step to reducing wasteful water consumption. "Public Space for Social Functions" links together two themes that surfaced throughout this project – the importance of public space and the importance of civil society, and the positive impact that the creation of the former with water can have in fostering the latter. "Responsible Ecology" obviously puts forth broad suggestions for harnessing the natural qualities of water as well as other constituent urban elements as prominent tools with which to create a new cityscape. Responsible ecology, however, valorizes the idea that the first true step to sustainability lies in personal and social responsibility. The final current of "Design Theories for the Future City" comprises broad proposals that offer a theoretical paradigm for coherent, collaborative, interdisciplinary, and humanistic urban design. The manifesto is an educational document but not a didactic one. It aims to liberate thinking and provoke new ideas. It does not seek to dictate. It speaks overwhelmingly to the policy level while using some examples based on case studies or unique project proposals to make its point. It is, then, a strategic and not a tactical document. My work here does not enter into a discussion of implementation nor does it suggest legislative, regulatory, or technical steps for execution. Rather, it is a provider of ideas on a global scale, and an incubator for more detailed technical and tactical ideas that can be further investigated, applied, and carried out by interested citizens, policymakers, and other researchers. The arguments I have put forth are not economically driven, nor do they purport to be. However, the proposed direction of the manifesto would not be cost-intensive to pursue. On the contrary, for a city that is aiming to transform itself (in large part by 2015 to meet the deadline for hosting Expo), my proposals are reasonable from a cost-benefit perspective and practical in terms of execution. The Milanese territory is changing and has chosen to change. Given this, a manifesto that encourages a plurality of stakeholders and levels of government to work more collaboratively and effectively together; educates citizens to waste less water and energy; and puts forth an intellectual framework for designers and architects to create public assets that are socially responsive and ecologically responsible, is in fact something that encourages improved stewardship of public resources. Considering that more effective government means less money spent on 'red tape,' savings can be reclaimed through reduced energy and water waste. Moreover, high-quality infrastructures that are responsive to the city's hydrological, environmental and user needs result in greater uptake and use by the civic population, have longer life spans, and require less regular maintenance. All of this leads to Milan being a more livable and better-managed city. This, in turn, improves the city's reputation and "brand" and demonstrates to the world that Milan is not the disorderly, grey, aquatically challenged, and civically bereft place that detractors claim it to be. A large part of my thesis research involved interviews with over twenty researchers, designers and practitioners working in the fields of water policy, urban hydrology, and urban design, including several Domus Academy faculty members and the MUVAD program director. My conversations with our program director in the fall of 2011 yielded an idea that continues to resonate with me. We talked about creating a new policy and governance plan for the city – but one for Milan's water as opposed to physical territory – a "piano di governo dell'acqua." The more I consider this notion, the more it makes sense[7]. I believe that failing to include water as a key element of the piano di governo del territorio[8] was a major weakness of this document. I would rather, then, like to think of a future piano di governo dell'acqua as a document that could be guided by my research, governed by the intellectual principles expressed through the manifesto, and then populated with the great volume and diversity of projects, ideas, machines, interventions, designs, plans, maps, et cetera, that are ideated in this larger volume and in the MUVAD 2010-2011 corpus. To be clear, however, the manifesto is not a piano di governo dell'acqua. It has not been converted into a white paper for thorough and intense public scrutiny and input. It has not been developed through a public engagement process involving thousands of people, and it has not been seen by either local or regional governments. Therefore, this manifesto, its research and its history could lay the groundwork for a future piano di governo dell'acqua, but the demands of creating such a complex document lay beyond the scope of this project and beyond its financial, temporal, and human resource capacities. This shall thus be work for another day, but I do hope that our efforts here can perhaps lay the groundwork for a future endeavour to provide comprehensive policy direction and

7. Gianandrea Barreca, Interview with Sean Yam, Recorded personal interview, Milano, October 2, 2011.; See also Gianandrea Barreca, "Ipotesi (realistiche) per riportare l'acqua a Milano," Linkiesta (Milano), June 25, 2011, http://www.linkiesta.it/ipotesi-realistiche-riportare-l-acqua-milano (accessed June 30, 2011).
8. During the period in which I wrote this thesis, the City of Milan's main strategic plan that was in the final phases of consultation was the Piano di Governo del Territorio headed up by the local architecture and urban design studio, Metrogramma. In my analysis, this document detrimentally ignored the role of water in the future development of the city. Regardless, with the election of a new local administration in the spring of 2011, the Metrogramma document has since been set aside and a new strategic plan developed. Metrogramma, Piano di Governo del Territorio (PGT), Milano: Comune di Milano, 2005, in The Plan, #47 (December 2010/January 2011), 38-93.

STRATEGY

planning guidelines for the morphology and hydrology of the city. If the final vision of my analysis is one where water becomes the true matrix of the city, where it is always a key consideration of policy and planning decisions, where it is respected, managed, and used responsibly by citizens and governments alike, and where the relationship amongst all the actors who have a stake in water is reciprocal, then in a future scenario where the manifesto will have had a real impact on the operations and daily life of Milan, I could envision:

- A new permanent, multi-stakeholder and intergovernmental agency overseen by a citizen board of directors that is tasked with managing all the metropolitan Milanese water systems on an integrated basis;
- Persuasive and memorable public service advertisements (via print media, television, internet, social media, billboards, etc.) throughout the Milanese territory educating people about water;
- A statistically demonstrable reduction in the consumption of bottled water and in the domestic and industrial consumption of potable water for non-potable purposes;
- New micro-interventions employing the aesthetics of water being placed in public areas of the city (*Img. 6/7*);
- New maps of Milan highlighting the presence and importance of water and encouraging local residents and visitors alike to engage with water;
- Urban voids such as underused parking lots, and abandoned industrial and transportation sites being converted into small-scale urban farms, solar farms, and bioremediation and phytoremediation centres;
- New and expanded green sites making use of all surface types and in the process equalizing ground water levels;
- Water being the main pillar of an international promotional campaign for Milan (for Expo 2015, for example).

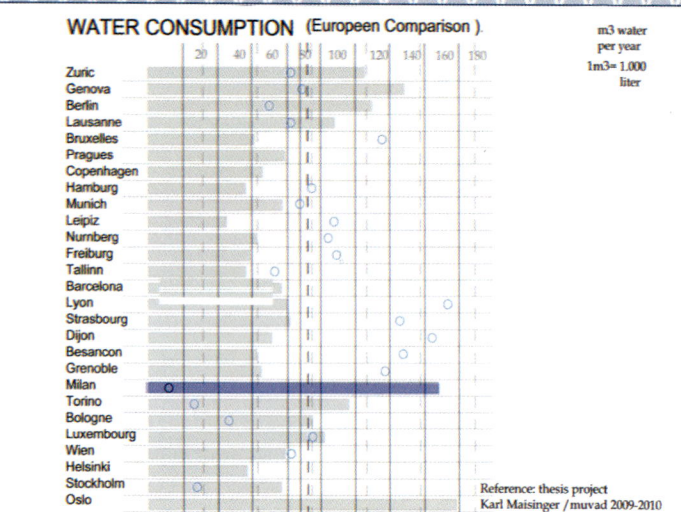

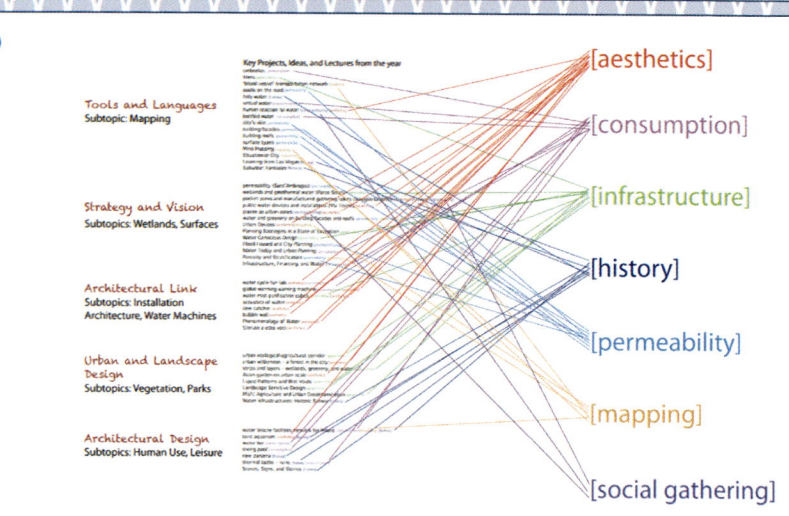

Img. 1 - Water consumption rates in Milan relative to other European cities.
Img. 2 - Mapping the major ideas and themes of the MUVAD 2010-2011 oeuvre by Sean Yam.
Img. 3 - The aesthetics of water for social interaction and quiet contemplation in the city.
Image by: Hideaki Nishimura, project: Triadic Water Concerto - Final Master project -2011.
Img. 4 - A schematic representation of the various vertical liquid and solid layers of the city.
Project title: Parco Solari by Alia Omari, Charbel Attieh - 2011.

STRATEGY

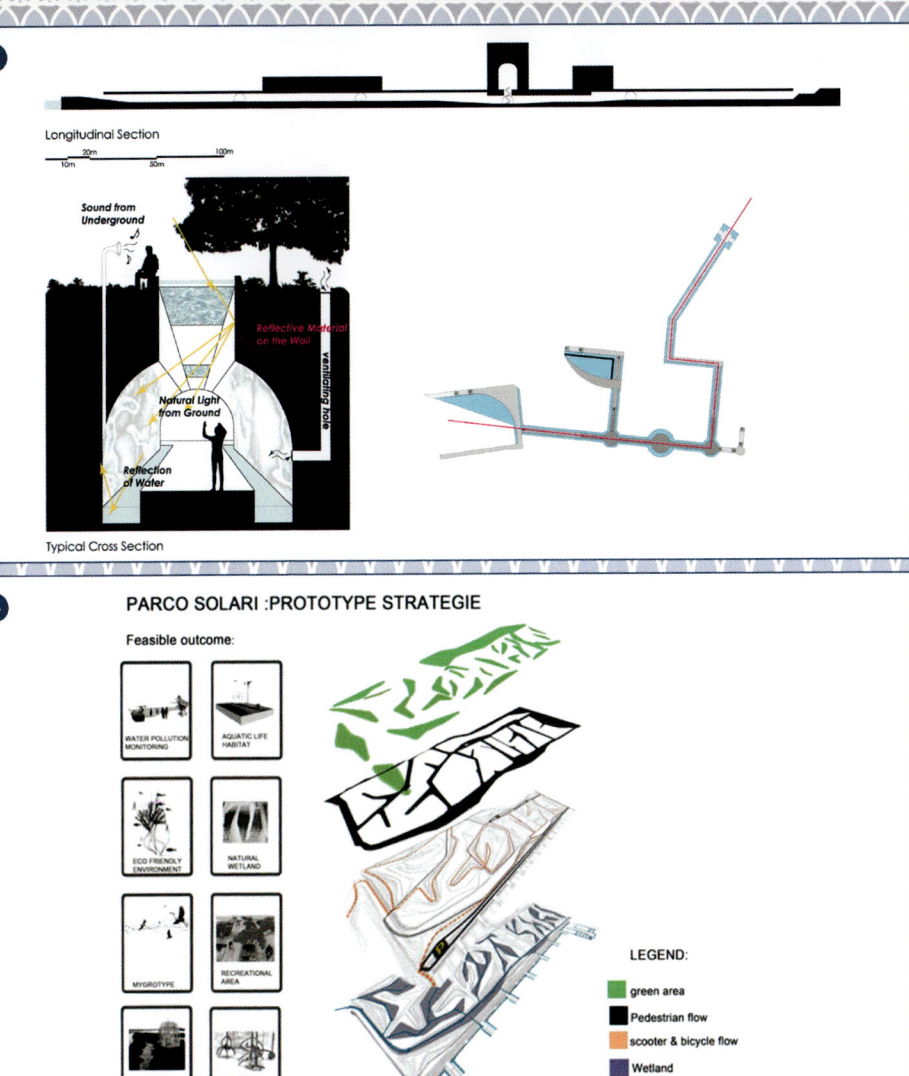

⑤ Tabula aquae benedictae
Architectural and Social Typologies of Holiness vis-à-vis Holy Water in Central Milanese Parish Churches

《《 Mapping Milan

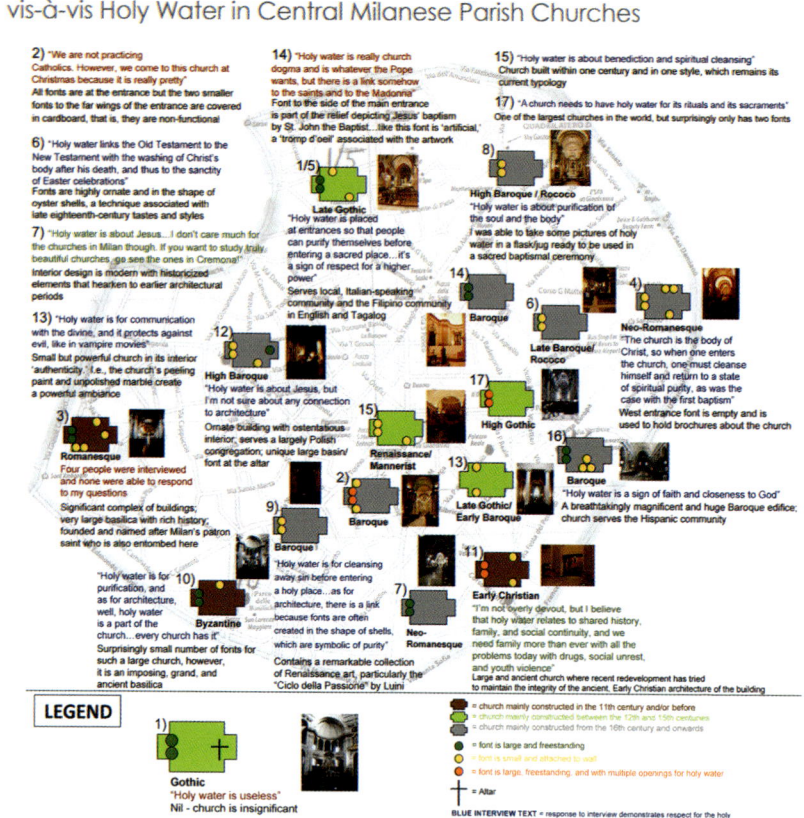

Img. 5 - New types of maps to understand better the cultural and hydrological assets of Milan, in this case, the architectural history of central parish churches vis-à-vis holy water by Sean Yam.
Img. 6 - A hypothetical public micro-intervention employing the aesthetics of water, in this case along the Naviglio Grande in Milan by Sean Yam.
Img. 7 - A hypothetical public micro-intervention employing the aesthetics of water, in this case along the Naviglio Grande in Milan by Sean Yam.

STRATEGY

S. YAM 045

Vast territories, minute gestures:
planning commencing with water

1. Introduction through images

Picture 1

In the centre of Milan the symbol of the city, adopted by his lordship, stands out: a large snake which historians often trace back to the power of the lords crushing their enemy. In fact, a fresh and neutral glance upon the image shows a man, or rather a child, who often smiles and dances, who appears to protrude out of the mouth of this large snake. Placing it alongside other images of cultures from distant times and lands, this representation appears to describe a civilisation which emerges from the powerful underground forces of deep waters, to be acknowledged and well managed, where possible, so that human life is possible.[9]

There are so many of these images, located in the most symbolic and strategic places of the lower plains - where the waters of high mountain glaciers resurface with ease – which, from this perspective, seem to clearly delineate the peculiarity and nature of this place: situated in one of the most fertile countrysides in the world boasting an enviable widespread presence of water. The water from the plain of springs facilitates cultivation, establishes and maintains cities.

Picture 2

During the making of a short film, in collaboration with Francesca Cogni[10], this territory was travelled following the flow of its waters: a different way of crossing the hard and edified ground, in which seemingly distant places unexpectedly and often invisibly connect with one another. Upon arriving at a farmhouse, situated just south of Milan, to film a water meadow - a wise cultivation system that allows forage to be cut several times a year - the farmer told us that there was no water that day.

He rode his moped through the streets of the centre and we followed him by car, following flows that were unknown to us, but which were clear to him, interceptable under manholes otherwise invisible to unsuspecting passers-by. Here is where clean waters flow and fish live. Sometimes setbacks can occur, as we discovered that day: an obstruction in a duct situated underground among offices, shops and universities, had interrupted the water flow suppling the water meadow, kilometres below. The farmer resurfaced from the manhole downhearted because of the interruption, but happy to have located it (*Img. 2*).

---

9. Cfr. P. Lembi, "Il fiume sommerso: Milano, le acque, gli abitanti", Jaca Book, Milan 2006.
10. Cfr. il film di Francesca Cogni e Pietro Lembi, "Ephemeroptera – gesti sull'acqua " (2007).

Picture 3

Stories and legends of Milan which are so beautiful that I am afraid to actually check "their truth", tell of a small lake situated under the Duomo of Milan, accessible by boat: "my grandfather saw it", "a friend of a friend told me about it"... Words that describe a widespread feeling among the Milanese relating to a sensation of sailing or at least standing above majestic waters on which the very stability of their buildings depends. Whilst filming, we met the employee of the factory of the Duomo, who several times a week, drops a probe into three manholes and notes the level of the aquifer in his notebook. A thousand-year old link to an underground rock from which our drinking water is extracted everyday (*Img. 3*).

Picture 4

Un/awareness of all of this. People queuing up in front of the "water distributors". It is true that one of the two taps supplies water mixed with carbon dioxide. However, I do not think that this mass presence derives primarily from this. Rather from the "story" of water. The municipal authorities have decided to demonstrate that water from the aqueducts, the water which millions of residents "miraculously" have access to from their own homes by simply opening a tap, is good and drinkable. The citizens rediscover this message, they appreciate it and share it. By queuing up (*Img. 4*).

2. Images and water

To envisage the places we live in filled with water flowing in and out (the apartment, the building, the city), to see them as they are, allowing for millions of metres of pipes to be glimpsed at, is just as difficult as "enlightening". To be able to explain the complexity and force of water which pours onto the Milanese territory, from the Alps and clouds, into different sources (springs, torrents, rivers, canals) according to a dense and inextricable but unobvious network (Milan does not have a big river), is even more difficult to describe. To intercept and govern this system is an enormous task. This is related to policies (hydraulic, agricultural, environmental, etc.) and urban planning, as well as to the culture of its inhabitants, the anthropology of its places and to our lives today. The actions performed by the farmers that interweave geometries between the countryside and the places beneath the manholes of the city, (and even the actions carried out by the campè, those involved in the management of the water, now almost extinct ...); the tasks carried out by the person responsible for surveying

the aquifer; and the gestures of citizens who always approach fountains (the green dragon…) and the countless other taps in the city, to drink and wash, in addition to many other water places to play, to contemplate, and even swim and sail…
Like mayflies, these gestures indicate the presence of water. These small insects, whose Greek name means "short-lived", live their first phase of life (preimaginal) in water. The adults, known as "imago", emerge above the water and generally live less than a day. Like these ephemeral and delicate insects, which hover over water and indicate its presence, the actions of the many actors in our daily lives come into contact, reside and indicate the invisible waters of the city; they invade them or lightly brush against them next to other living beings. From the minute gestures repeated by millions of inhabitants who are a billion times in contact with this imposing presence, to the decisions made by professionals, who need to know and regulate this system. In the following pages, I will try to describe, step by step, a selection of issues currently related to planning practice with reference to water, starting from the personal experience gained over the years in various fields.

3. Maps, glances, blindness

During certain months of the year, when the fields of Milan are illuminated by reflections from the rice fields, the imposing presence of water in this area becomes more apparent (*Img. 5*). The network of canals, irrigation ditches, canals, rivers, torrents, diverters, pipes and springs is actually still very impressive today, though often invisible in our daily lives and in the same planning regulations (*Img. 6*). Gradually increasing from the late nineteenth century, water has since several decades almost disappeared from urban maps to make room for other elements: buildings drawn in detail, roads and railways. By simply looking back in time, it is apparent that, for obvious reasons (military defence, transportation, supplies, etc.), rivers and canals were the main elements on maps: often exaggerated, they emerged as the main protagonist in the representations of the territory (*Img. 7/8*). In conjunction with this particular blindness, urban planning generally struggles to clearly share, and effectively express itself on the matter. Outside the regulations and sectoral policies (management of drinking water and drainage systems, hydraulic cleaning, etc.) a common language seems to be missing within the entire territorial planning and even more so in the social body as a whole. Territories have generally turned their backs on waterways during the twentieth century. Milan itself has erased its internal canals carried away by the speed of new means of transport and by an ideology typical of sanitary engineering. Today, many Administrations are turning their thoughts towards these places of water. On the whole, I believe it is still an uncertain glance, which seeks functions that restore meaning (tourism, leisure, sustainable transport …), but which alone do not appear to be enough for such a "revolution", starting with the water that has marked certain periods of the millenary history of Milan and its neighbouring territories.

4. Policies, projects, actions

In recent years, much has been said of the Milanese waters on a technical level and by the general public (local referendum for the restoration of the Darsena and the re-opening of the system of canals in Milan, the Expo Waterway project, etc.). Meetings and reports and projects have been prepared.

The policies in line with European Directives (Water Framework Directive 2000/60/EC, Flood Risk Directive 2007/60/EC) and with national legislation (L. 183/89, L.D. 152/99) strive to protect the quality and balance of the water cycle, as well as to protect the environment and ecosystems concerning water bodies, with a view to addressing these issues in relation to the scale of river /drainage basins:

A number of sector plans (Drainage Basin Management Plan, Protection and use of water Programme, Severance Plan for Hydrogeological Assessment, etc.) identify measures, addresses, objectives and actions.

Attempts are made to connect to the territories by drawing up sub-basin projects required by the regional planning law (Italian Regional Law 12/2005 Art. 55-bis) which recognises suitable territorial areas for the management of water and soil in the sub-basins, in order to pursue objectives such as the management of territorial transformation processes, the integration of regional and local policies, the containment and reduction of landscape and environmental degradation.

There are many plans and projects which are related to the water system and territories on different territorial scales. Many institutional levels and parties are also involved (Lombardy Region, Local Authorities, River Basin Authorities, Interregional Agency for the Po River, private consortiums, etc.).

It is impossible to visualise the many available actions (policies, constraints, plans and projects) in just one image. The table below lists just a few of them: these vary from the Regional Territorial Plan of the Lombardy Navigli Area (instrument involving 51 municipalities regarding protection objectives, enhancement and requalification not only of the canals but also of the landscape in which they are situated), to various higher-level constraints (Italian Legislative Decree 42/04 - Code of Cultural Heritage and Landscape, Bands specified in the Severance Plan for Hydrogeological Assessment [Piano stralcio per l'Assetto Idrografico - PAI], the Regional Landscape Plan [Piano Paesaggistico Regionale], Territorial Plan of the Provincial Coordination [Piano Territoriale di Coordinamento Provinciale], and others), to the Waterway project linked to Expo 2015, Regional River Parks and Local Parks of supra-municipal interest connected to the watercourses (*Img. 9*). Many actions are excluded from the table: municipal scale policies and projects, in addition to, for example, the measures scheduled in the River Agreements (Territorial Development Framework Agreements - Accordi Quadro di Sviluppo Territoriale AQST aimed at the requalification of river basins, undersigned by the Region, Local Administrations and other interested parties). The list could continue. However, to put it bluntly, the impression is given that all these policies, constraints and incentives not only do not seem to lead to a unified framework, but neither do they intercept the actual practice of those who set out urban plans nor the overall operations of local administrations. Despite good intentions or integration objectives between policies, highly specialised sectoral policies which struggle to communicate with the more general governing of the territory too often govern the waters at all institutional levels. Conversely, despite the impressive amount of studies, plans and proposals, water still appears to be significantly invisible to urban policies, which claim "ignorance" in the face of its presence and the forms and problems created by the same. Rather than drawing them closer, it would appear that this wealth of plans, resources, expertise, institutional sectors, agreements, etc., pushes the waters even further away from our territories. Blindness was mentioned earlier: perhaps it is the absence of feeling or clearly perceiving the water bodies as a vital and fundamental presence in every civilisation and age and therefore also in ours.

In national and regional policies, for example, the importance of an approach to planning which begins from the sub-basins can be recognised, but then it becomes very difficult to express this vision in the actual planning practice. Alternatively, the importance of the irrigation system for agricultural purposes can still be stated, however municipal planning in practice often struggles to focus on this theme, often even contradicting it.

This shortfall, which affects the technical sphere, has to do mostly with poor dialogue between the offices of the same public administrations and between different disciplines: a dialogue that certainly needs to be reinforced - when not built from scratch – by using various forms, including that of training able to affect also organisational cultures within the Public Administrations. This directly concerns efficient forms of governance, often self-referential, between territorial parties and sectoral policies.

5. Feel the waters

However, there is perhaps a more general aspect concerning the current collective perception of water and the ability of society as a whole to make it a spatial and territorial project, with social, cultural and economic values.

As already mentioned, we do not presently appear to be in one of those phases which have marked the history of the territories between the Ticino and Adda and between the Lakes and the Po over the centuries, creating remarkable spatial and urban revolutions based on the promotion of water: by providing an overall and powerful shape to the land based on important works from a material and "imaginative" point of view. This does not occur for different reasons, which I can summarise with the words "the absence of necessity". If, in the past, the primary and fundamental need to obtain water for everyday life or to provide water for agriculture, transport or for military defence was strongly felt by society at large, or at least by those who had the capability and the legitimacy to implement policies governing the territory, today this need is not transmitted with the same energy. Many of these functions are still needed (drinking clean water, irrigating the fields, etc.), but do not seem to possess that feature of "ordered necessity" for which a society decides to shape the territory, starting by caring for its waters.The planning of residential, productive and commercial functions follows its paths, while at the same time the policies focused on hydraulics and water quality, pursue their objectives in a specialised way. In this context, often the only projects in which the territory is modified with particular attention to the water system, focus on accessory functions (forgive the term): bike paths, ecological corridors, places of entertainment for citizens tired from long working hours and from being in very restricted spaces; overly attentive, often biased and nostalgic, local operations (but water teaches us that it emerges in specific points, but comes from afar).

These are important dimensions but which, I think, do not reach the heart of the matter.They do not allow for planning (the whole territory and its places) starting from its waters.How do you allow the water system to come to light, to be narrated and to be shaped, so that it speaks to the different generations and not only to the Milanese, but to the world? How to proceed so that existing but also very ancient artefacts can be relied on, and how can bold and real questions be answered (for example, to provide continuity to the waters of Milan, to those of the west with those of the east, those of the north with those in the south) by searching for and creating new unexpected objects which are able to impress. How to create unique places starting from the force of water and its often very light voice, so as to weave together the water cycle with new technologies, accessible public spaces and environmental and economic sustainability, according to contemporary needs.

It seems to me that the proposals stimulated in recent years within the Master in Urban Vision and Architectural Design, strive to indicate directions, by gathering different points of views, by addressing these issues from very different angles, by highlighting the contributions of people who come from different cultures and distant countries, by creating workshops with participants bringing heterogeneous disciplines and practices. Stimuli and seeds, for an urban planning practice which is often tired and barren (*Img. 10*).

Img. 1 - **Mermaid made of white Carrara marble, by Giuseppe Franchi** - The Fountain of Verziere (G. Piermarini, 1782), made of pink granite of Baveno: powered by the waters of the Seveso, it was the first public fountain in Milan (photo by P. Lembi).
Img. 2 - **Piazza del Duomo ("Cathedral Square") in Milan**: big snake, emblem on the Archbishop's Palace (photo by P. Lembi).
Img. 3 - **Piazza del Duomo ("Cathedral Square") in Milan**: periodic survey of the height of the aquifer (photo by P. Lembi).
Img. 4 - **Water House in San Giuliano Milanese** (photo by P. Lembi).
Img. 5 - **Reflections in the rice paddies of the City of Milan - Trenno / Gallarate, May 2013** (photo by P. Lembi).
Img. 6 - **Water system-SIT PIM Studies Center, from different sources** (Geoportal Lombardy Region, Reclamation Consortium Est Ticino Villoresi, Province of Milan and others).

052 STRATEGY

P. LEMBI

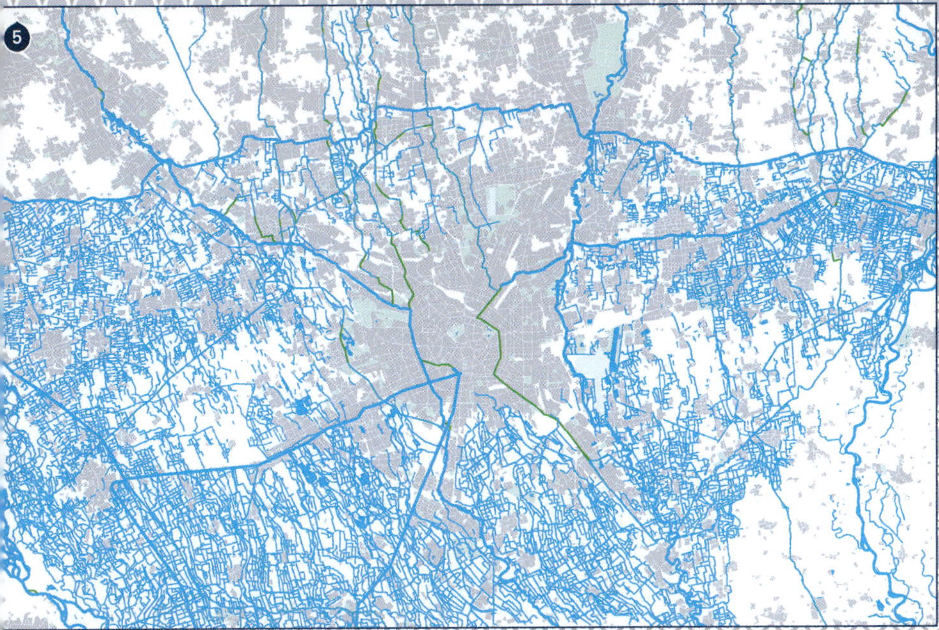

053

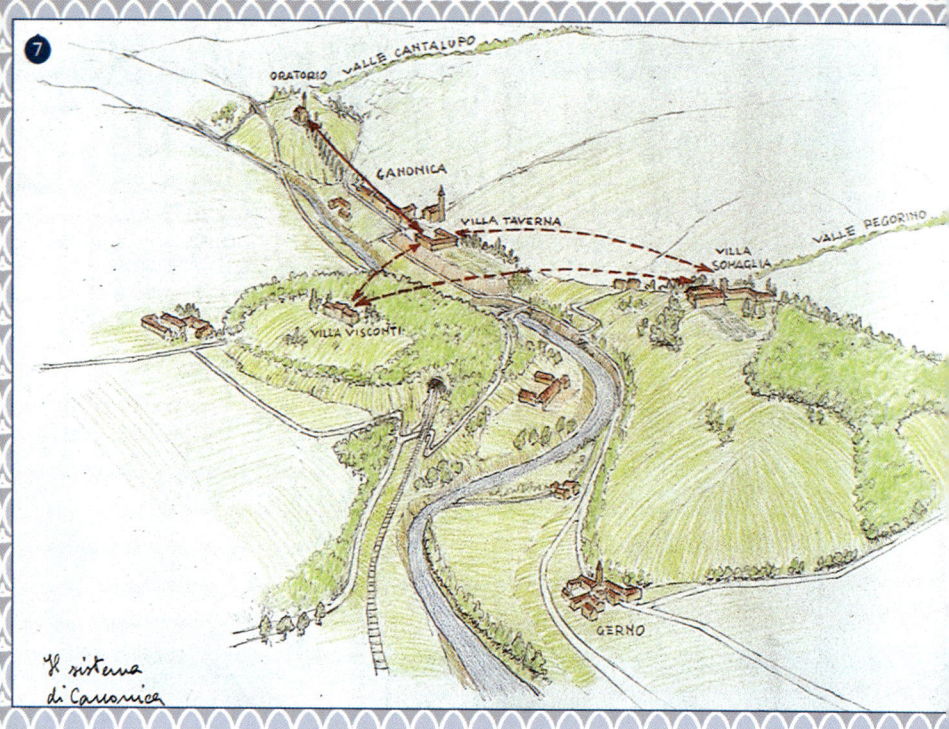

Imgs. 7/8 - **Drawings taken from the Province of Milan, PIM Studies Center, "Project Lambro," 1989. In them observation and hand drawing are trying to bring out "the consistency of water" and their relationship with the environment: a quality often lost in the current zoning boards.**

054 STRATEGY

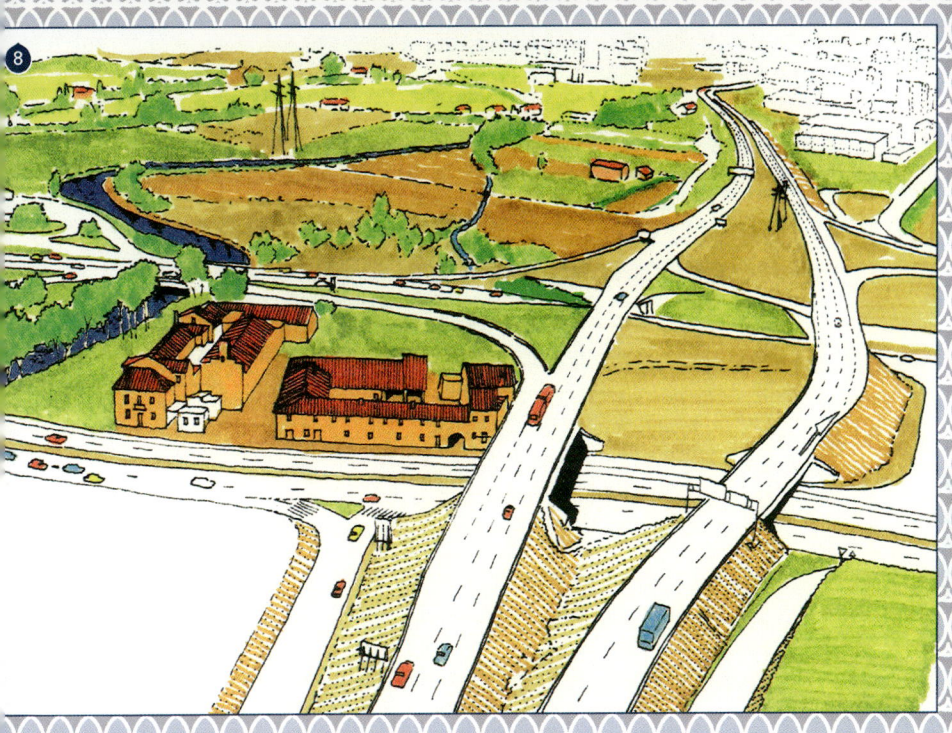

P. LEMBI

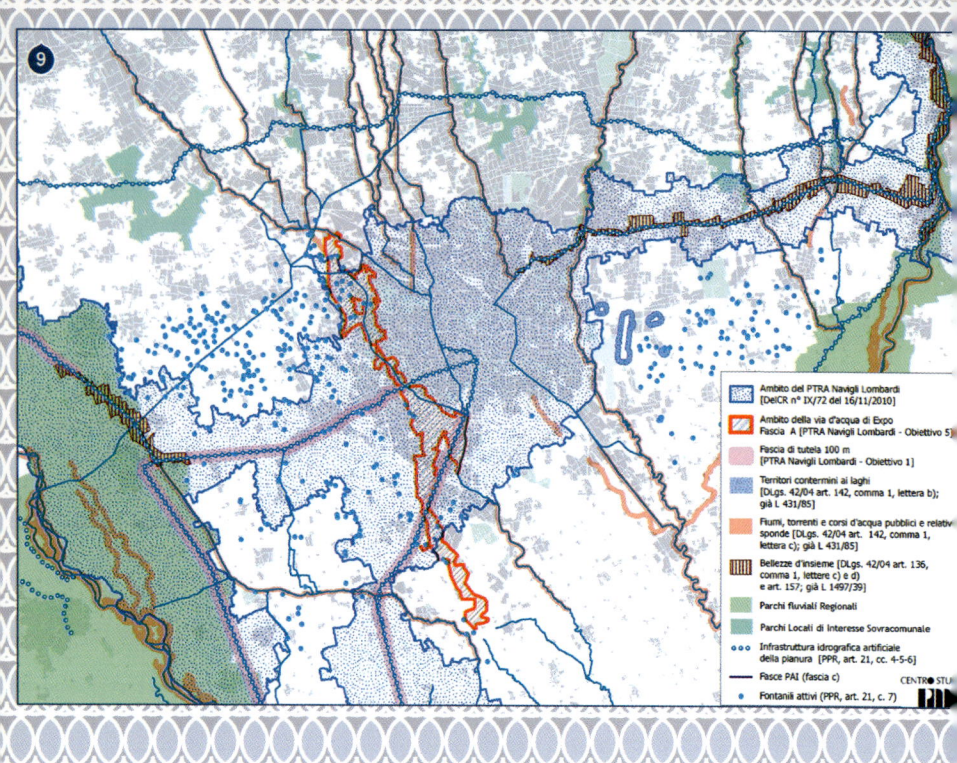

Img. 9 - Some of policies, actions and constraints related to the water system (PIM Studies Center, 2013).
Imgs. 10/11 - Water reflections: never the same, always the same, beyond every administrative and disciplinary border (photo by P. Lembi).

STRATEGY

P. LEMBI

CONNECTION

Water Connections/Urban veins

Opening the tap, flushing the toilet, showering. All these actions are part of our daily life. There is hardly any building that is not served by the water supply, and different sewage systems guarantee the smooth process of the washing away of liquid and odour. Drainage and water collection systems, such as gutters and manholes, are just little visible objects of the complex system of water management. These elements together with dykes, bridges and controlling elements are easy to see and recognize in the urban landscape. They represent a collection of devices that escape our gaze which is used, bored, accustomed to their presence. People are used to water, and only during water crises, such as exceptional drought or flooding, they do start to question these systems, and the ways in which they cross the urban environment. The nowadays urban scenario is part of this relatively recent evolution. It is only from the late Eighteen Century that European cities changed their relation with the water system. As Sennett points out "European cities began cleaning, draining holes and swampy depressions filled with urine and faeces, pushing dirt into sewers below the street. The very street surface changed in this effort. In the middle of the eighteenth century the English began to pave London using flat, squared granite flagstones; the streets could then be cleaned more thoroughly; below them, urban veins replaced shallow cesspools, the sewers in Paris carrying dirty water and excrement to the new sewage canals"[11]. In urban environments water connections can be considered as the spaces that control the water flow. They secretly affect landscapes, buildings, and the relation between human and the resource.

There are mainly two typologies of connections: the first one consists of superficial watercourses, rivers, channels and natural flow-systems, the second one refers to the "piped" system, applied systematically on the urban scale and later, on the regional scale. Both systems together constitute the urban infrastructure of supply and drainage of water, where infrastructure is meant as the network through what the flood flows and the resource is distributed. While the piped system's notion did not evolved from its originally appointed function and its relation with the city remained unaltered, the natural water system's notion profoundly mutated within the urban environment during the Industrial Revolution. The superficial watercourses cross the city through a complex system of channels and natural reservoirs that due to gravity are linked to more important rivers all belonging to the urban systems. The existing non-artificial water network is a natural mean for the distribution of water, when deep enough is used as transport system, and, in absence of other networks, becomes a natural collector of garbage and sewage. In conjunction with urban concentration and population growth, and in presence of particular conditions, (i.e. weather), the water's environment easily collapse. Because of these circumstances, progressively,

11. Sennett, *Flesh and Stone*, 263.

the urgency to get rid of foul smell and waste, the fear for flooding, together with the upcoming necessity of providing more space for the transport network, built up the idea of covering all the minor water systems, with prompt construction of artificial draining channels and road surfacing, and to control the river through constructions of artificial banks. Fear perceived in relation to natural water flows, polluted and uncontrolled, is balanced by the growing feeling of desire for the artificial piped water system and by technological devices that would re establish order, and cleanliness, not only in the urban environment, but in the broad sense, to the city "of the dreadful night"[12]. The underground placement of channels and rivers, the fear for water, the function of the river as main interceptor of all the waste of the city together with the progressive mutation of the city through an industrial system where water was of primary importance because factories and commercial businesses needed large quantities of water and easy discharge systems, not only changed people's perception of water courses but also the idea of the landscapes close to the water networks. Before the Industrial Revolution, rivers hosted "social" spaces as collection of water, wash of clothes; after that, on the contrary, pollution and the new functions as "noxious trades" made that impossible, and river became preferable sites for the settlement of some of the most fragile population.

The transformation of superficial watercourses through all hydraulic and engineeristic adaptations can be defined as an attempt to "tame nature" or as stated by Swyngedouw: "the urbanisation process itself became predicated on the mastering and engineering nature's waters[13]".

As in the spaces for production of water, all the hydraulic works were embraced with a sense of power to nature, and the idea that modernity was coming in the shape of water control systems. The second typology of these socio-spatial spaces is related to the underground piped system, either for providing and discharging water. The piped system carries out the supply and drainage of water through various systems of pipes that cross the city and are mostly buried underground or within buildings. . The two piped systems are aqueducts and sewers. Pipes connect the spaces of water production (through water works where water is controlled, chlorinated, and put in pressure) to the final users through a series of different pipes (main, secondary, etc., up to the domestic connections). They generally lay underground, connected to the street level by a series of gutters. If not pressurized, structures for water provision are basically at the ground level or elevated, as they have to use gravity to provide pressured water.

The aqueduct's dimension is based on the quantity of water needed for each inhabitant, that progressively grew from of an estimated the amount of water per capita between 7 and 20 litres (up to 30 litres if water was used to wash the streets and clothes) between 1750 and 1850, to 200 litres per capita, with no distinction between drinking

12. Peter Hall, Cities of Tomorrow: An Intellectual History of Urban Planning and Design in the Twentieth Century, 3rd Edition (Wiley-Blackwell, 2002).

13. Swyngedouw, «Power, nature, and the city. The conquest of water and the political ecology of urbanization in Guayaquil, Ecuador», 321.

water and water for domestic uses[14], at the beginning of the Twentieth century, to an estimated need per capita of 200 litres/per person/per day[15] in the present situation. The possibility to withdraw water from a distant place, to pump it through pressurized system underground, and mathematic calculation of the estimate need per capita, erase the specificity of the site's environmental conditions namely geomorphology, the kind of settlement, the capacity to find local resources; the city progressively is considered as a flat, uncharacterized "unicum" to be served, or as Boyer's defines "the metropolis was believed to be an inorganic and fabricated environment, the product of mathematics and the creation of the engineer"[16], to be controlled and managed. Urban environments, starting from the rolling down of networks, are perceived as a tabula rasa, ready to be modified, put into the grid, connected, tamed and forged by the "technological sublime". The variation of the architecture of the infrastructure also changed the perception of the water's sources. In the Roman Empire aqueducts were up-ground infrastructures cutting the city's sections, made usually with arches, thus visible objects in the landscape. Aqueducts were usually named after Emperors that ordered the infrastructures' works (Acqua Marcia from Quinto Marcio Re) and with characteristics of the water carried (Aqua Tepula, from Colli Albani took its name from the warmth of its water, Anio Vetus and Anio Novus, from the Aniene river). The naming system immediately connected citizens to the source of water, raising awareness on the places water was withdrawn. As water is buried underground, it loses its connection from the source. The only architectures connected to the water systems are water towers, which work as a pressure point for the network.

The whole distance from the source of water, the relative ease to get water, the unknown connections all enhanced the idea that water is a free and unlimited resource. The piped sewage system is more complex than the water supply system, because of the technological characteristics, the physical spaces it generates, and the way it is perceived by the users/inhabitants of the city. As well as aqueducts for waterworks, there is an evolution from a single-standing system composed by cesspools, privy vaults, pit latrines to a connected system, piped and buried underground. Spread of sewage is slower than aqueducts. The first reason is related to the difficulty to get funds simultaneously for waterworks and sewage, as they both require big starting capitals. At the same time profit for water works, as Gerhard[17], states, is associated to the taxpayers that are more willing to pay for water works, while it is harder to get revenue for the sewage system. The second reason is the idea that sewage system is not of primary concern and necessity compared to the water supply, and the idea is enhanced by the possibility of using different disposal methods on site (privy vault and cess pits). The sudden population growth, and the overcrowding conditions drive

14. Goubert, The Conquest of Water, 52.
15. Average daily water consumption pro capita in Italy (Istituto Ambiente 2007).
16. M. Christine Boyer, The City of Collective Memory: Its Historical Imagery and Architectural Entertainments (The MIT Press, 1996), 116.
17. Sanitation and sanitary engineering : Gerhard, William Paul, 1854-: Free Download & Streaming: Internet Archive, 99, consultato Febbraio 20, 2012, http://www.archive.org/details/sanitationandsa01gerhgoog.

CONNECTION

to a quick and over filling of cesspits and privy vaults, while the overall situation is complicated by the increase of the use of water, enhanced by the new technologies of water supply. As Melosi describes, analysing the advent of water networks in United States and implication to the sewage, "privy vaults and cesspools could not contend with a water-delivery system that increased volume so dramatically. It was the environmental implications of this clash of technologies that provided momentum for change. Flooding problems, and especially threats to health, were directly traceable to the breakdown of the pre-sewer systems. Yards inundated with wastes became new battlegrounds for programs of environmental sanitation"[18]. Two kinds of sewers were implemented by the end of the Nineteenth century and still in use, separate and combined systems. The two systems differ in the separation between the storm water and human wastewater (separate system) with a combined system that does not separate the two discharged waters. Usually the combined system was applied to medium-large cities, where the costs of two separate systems were too high to be afforded, while in small cities, where the storm water system was not compulsory to be put underneath, the separate system was applied[19]. Sewers are perceived as something inaccessible, far, chaotic and dangerous tool for waste management. This perception is due to the fact that people don't see any more the flow of the water, but imagine the foul and dangerous materials flowing within the artificial veins. They can be interpreted as "complex intersection between the human body and the built environment"[20] or as the connection between the upcoming and newly introduced private space in the house and the blurred, uncontrolled urban space, the space between buildings. They represent "a point of reference for the complex labyrinth of connections that bind urban space into a coherent whole, being one of the most intricate and multi-layered symbols and structures underlying the modern metropolis"[21]. Pipes represent, pipes represent a symbol of modernity, because they "literally carr(ied) the idea of progress into the urban domain and providing the confirmation that the road to a better society was under construction and paved with networks"[22], but "once completed, the networks became buried underground, invisible, rendered banal and relegated to an apparently marginal, subterranean urban underworld[23], thus becoming "background for other kinds of work"[24].

18. Melosi, The Sanitary City, 62.
19. There is a huge academic debate about the two systems. Since the first conceive of the sewage, with Hausmann and Belgrand debating in Paris and Chadwick and Balzagette in London, the separation of the faecaes from the storm water is an open problem. The challenges were relating to the economic importance of the human waste as fertilizer, sold to the country; by the resistance made by the night scavengers, and cessipt cleaning companies whose job was put in risk by the new technology and by the fear of contaminating "clean" water and the underground city. The rising use of water together with high costs for a new network that would collect the human waste finally made the predominant choice of combining the two wastewater.
20. Matthew Gandy, «Rethinking urban metabolism: water, space and the modern city», City 8, n° 3 (Dicembre 2004): 363–379, doi:10.1080/136048104200 0313509.
21. Matthew Gandy, «The Paris Sewers and the Rationalization of Urban Space», Transactions of the Institute of British Geographers 24, n° 1 (Aprile 1, 1999): 24, doi:10.1111/j.0020-2754.1999.00023.x.
22. Kaika, City of Flows, 37–38.
23. Kaika e Swyngedouw, «Fetishizing the modern city», 121.
24. SUSAN STAR L., «The ethnography of Infrastructure», AMERICAN BEHAVIORAL SCIENTIST, 1999, SAGE edizione, par 43, 380.

M. C. PASTORE 063

Imgs. 1/2/3/4/5/6 - **Exploration of the Subterranean Sewage System in Milan. Pictures by Maria Chiara Pastore, 2012**

M. C. PASTORE

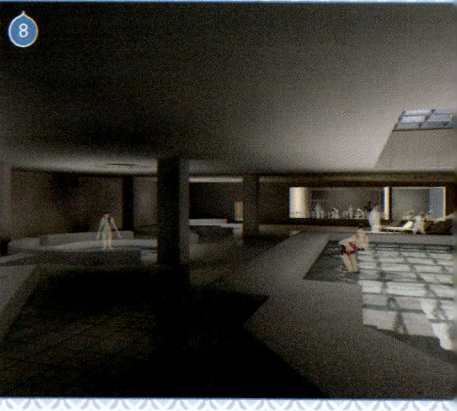

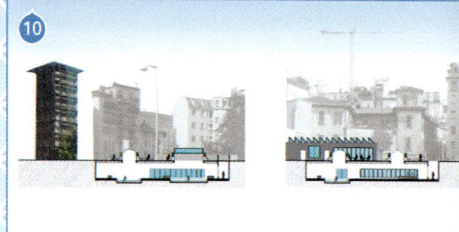

Imgs. 7/8/9/10 - Rediscovery water ruin - Project for a thermal spa complex in Milan - Chien-Sheng Pan
Img. 11 - Typological Analysis-Apparent Water. Project title: "Triadic water concerto" by - Hideaki Nishimura - Final Master Project 2011.
Img. 12 - Underground Waterways. Image of Underground Plaza - Plan Ground Level - Plan Underground Level by Hideaki Nishimura. Project: Triadic Water Concerto, Final Thesis, 2011.

M. C. PASTORE

Fluid systems for urban connections

In every culture, in every age and in every place, man has felt the need to relate to the territory around him and on which he settled, struggling to extend his control over nature. In the eternal conflict between harmony and predominance, between adapting to the needs and the force of nature, whilst controlling and managing the same, human activities and constructions have always, in the end, observed the specific and unique character of the environment in which they were created. Not always consistent, but always profoundly linked to the characteristics and essence of the landscape, human activities have basically outlined the relationship between man and the surrounding nature. Whether ideological, conflictual or even romantic, the shape and, often before this, meaning of our cities, is based on the need for nature and at the same time for the emancipation from the ties of nature.
Nevertheless, a revival in the relationship with natural elements has been taking place for many years now in several cities, in particular with water, which represents and constitutes a kind of synthesis. Notably, the relationship of Mediterranean coastal cities such as Barcelona, Genoa and Naples with the sea and in general with the water surrounding and crossing the built up areas of the same, has, in a sort of collective euphoria, been reconsidered and renewed.
Initially maritime, followed by fluvial or lacustrine waterfronts occupied, and still occupy, an important part of the debate on the necessary correct and harmonious development of these cities using this natural element. An element which cities measure themselves against and from which they have long drawn life, resources and inspiration.
There are also other cities, only a few in Europe, which apparently have no relation with water. Cities that neither have seas, rivers nor lakes. Milan is in large part one of these, or at least it appears today to be so, certainly by its external appearance.
A few rare traces of a past in which water was present and represented an important feature of the city, now often appear abandoned and left to their fate (*Imgs. 1/2*). There seems to be no clear strategy for them, no project for the future going beyond their "local" rehabilitation or urban maquillage.
In Milan in particular, water has never been a part, so to speak, of a natural environment. Unlike the sea, rivers or lakes, in Milan water always appears in the form of a mechanical fluid, a genuine part of the life and rhythms of the city.
It is hardly ever present as a decorative, free or spectacular element, but as a work-related element, closely connected to hydraulic engineering aimed at improving the efficiency of production systems in which water played an important role. Agriculture, for example, followed by manufacturing and then by heavy industries; these activities have always been closely linked and connected to the hydraulic system that characterised the area of Milan.

However, today, just a few traces remain of this great hydraulic machine that was once the city. Some are still visible, others have been erased or covered, but persist in the form of the city and are manifested through subtle clues, such as the locks (*Img. 3*). If, at the beginning of the twentieth Century, the decision was taken to cover the canals as a result of unhealthy water and a slow transport system, it is also true that the presence of water in the city contributed to Milan's primacy in agriculture at the beginning of the fifteenth Century and to the construction of its first major urban hospital (*Img. 4*). Is it worthwhile questioning the reopening of the canals today, especially their innermost parts, those belonging to part of the inner ring system? Perhaps a complete reopening cannot be envisaged, but certainly a talk and a project may be arranged in order to begin a partial and intermittent reopening. These activities would involve precise and coordinated actions performed with the archaeological care needed to dig up traces of the past, and the necessary attention to planning, casting new elements into the future, able to enrich urban spaces and signs of collective life. Why not take water from the Naviglio della Martesana to the covered square of the new skyscraper of the Lombardy Region? Why not take water from the millennial Roggia Vettabbia to the gardens around the hospital pavilions or in the courtyards of Ca'Granda? In other words, why not allow a new spatial experience between water and public space, which can relate to the places where Milan is changing and where it will build its own future identity? In the projects developed with the students, we have tried to focus our attention primarily on the theme of rediscovery and the potential that this rediscovery of water could have as a connecting system between today's seemingly separate and distant parts of the city. The projects reject the idea that water can only be used as a decorative element and implement a timely and surgical rediscovery of certain sections which may be capable of reactivating routes and reconnecting areas. The reopening of the canals could occur and be implemented in stages, primarily through a selection of certain segments only and certain objectives which may be interesting or brought to light, identified and reconnected to the life of the city. It has been extensively discussed and stated that, in order to give a sense of meaning to the whole system, that is the territorial system of canals, the inner ring of the canals needs to be reopened as a pivot for the whole system to rotate around, "like the spokes of a wheel"[1]. This does in fact seem logical, since the central ring is the natural place for all the water of a much wider territorial system to flow into. At the same time, however, this would imply a total revolution of the city's road system, not that this is impossible, but it would certainly be difficult, perhaps out of proportion compared to the results or the benefits that would derive from the same. Perhaps

1. Roberto Biscardini, "Navigli, 30 anni dopo Biscardini commenta Gianni Beltrame", from http:// www.riaprireinavigli.it/, 23 January 2013

rather than a revolution, which has never been accomplished entirely or in full in our country, in any historical period nor in any field of knowledge, it would be better to imagine a system made up of pieces, a slower and measured evolution (*Img. 5*). This would lead to a sense of acquired maturity, an awareness of one's own ability would be gained and would oblige future generations to acquire ownership and a need for continuous consideration and work.

These are operations, however, that are always restricted to areas of limited extent and characterised by interventions measured by the size of the works. A hidden hydraulic and urban system would be allowed to resurface and be brought to light through urban surgeries reopening closed ground (*Imgs. 6/7*). The projects on the whole enact a strategy on a greater scale and together, one after the other, rediscover and bring to light an important aspect of the city's structure by redeveloping an urban quality that has long been buried. The Conca del Naviglio, the Vettabbia, the Martesana in Via San Marco, are places which represent opportunities in which to experiment this rediscovery. Reopening and uncovering the hidden canal from under the asphalt and an infinite amount of cars, would create an extensive system of public space, arranged around the water. A system, which, unlike today, would not stop at the Darsena, but by going beyond the imaginary barrier of the Spanish walls, would extend towards the inner ring.

By reopening, for example, the stretch of via Conca del Naviglio, which could equally be done in other areas, would restore vitality to a pedestrian area of the city. It would enhance and bind together already consolidated urban systems, areas that are today practically hidden, such as those of the amphitheatre's gardens, and it would certainly build high quality, widespread and linear micro urban systems with a stronger character.

An extended water system and public space, specific for light and pedestrian traffic, would come into being, which, through the system of canals and the Darsena, would reach the inner ring (*Img. 8*).

The same operation could also be developed, for example, by rediscovering Vettabbia, becoming the connecting element for a system of green spaces such as gardens and parks, which, crossing the area of the former milk plant, could intercept the Ravizza Park and the area of the Bocconi University campus, continuing inland to link up with the last part of the Basilicas Park.

The same partial and measured operating method could be implemented by using other segments of the extensive network of underground canals to re-establish and reconnect existing disconnected urban and environmental systems.

The partial and selective reopening of the canals therefore becomes a real opportunity in order to contemplate the characteristics of the public space of our city. At the same time, it becomes a real opportunity to connect the now separated urban areas and to reconnect divided parts of cities, creating much wider urban systems. The reopening of the canals arranged through an overall strategic vision can certainly represent an opportunity to reflect on the construction of a new paradigm for the

design of urban space and the identification of its distinctiveness through the close relationship with the nature of the places. Therefore, as in the case of the Darsena and the segments of the canals that are still open, water could be an element of urban regeneration and the key requirement for the construction of a more extensive system of urban regeneration. A new, light and sophisticated urban ecological infrastructure that distributes positive energy and quality to areas that are today fragmented and separated. Only by rediscovering water and allowing it to play a role in the life of the city, in its peculiar and most interesting elements such as those of exchange and flow, will Milan be able to recognise this urban material once again as an integral and inseparable part of its identity. As Gianni Beltrame stated, the gradual redevelopment of some of its main branches which can be used for a variety of activities, appears possible, and can to some extent at least be understood by its citizens. According to some standards, Beltrame had already mapped out some functions in 1982, such as urban planning, connecting green areas, irrigation, navigation and leisure, including even energy production and fishing. These, complete the finished and ongoing rehabilitation of Naviglio Grande, Naviglio di Bereguardo, Naviglio Pavese, Naviglio di Martesana and Naviglio di Paterno (*Img. 9*). Within the debate, which has long been open on this issue, some are convinced that this partial rehabilitation of the external canals is neither sufficient nor coherent without the rehabilitation of the inner ring canal sections. In fact, much has been said on this issue in recent years following the outcome of a local referendum on whether or not to reopen the canals of the inner ring. Some research, projects and studies tend to insist that "by exploiting the five Canals, the five spokes of the wheel, without changing the centre pin of the spokes, this proposal has been confined to an area that still needed to be fully restored."[2]
It would therefore appear that, without the redevelopment of the "inner ring", the project could not be completed; an important activity in which citizens could have identified themselves. However, the outcome of the referendum must be read, in my opinion, in a broader sense. I prefer to interpret the outcome not as a demand for an "important project" but rather a useful project that incorporates a timely, widespread and pervasive reconnection strategy, which can be pursued and directed over time to the reappropriation of the city's themes and characteristics, which are currently lost and forgotten; hence the idea not to undertake a general project regarding the whole inner ring system with the students, but rather to explore where to intervene in order to reconnect and reorganise, through the resurfacing of water and its powerful sense of structure. The design exercise which has been developed gives voice, not only to and for Milan, to a renewed and increasingly wider desire towards reusing the collective assets present in the territory. Perhaps the only assets today which can be rediscovered and exploited well beyond the sole theme of their preservation.

2. Toti Celona, Gianni Beltrame, "I Navigli milanesi" edited by Province of Milan, Milan, 1982

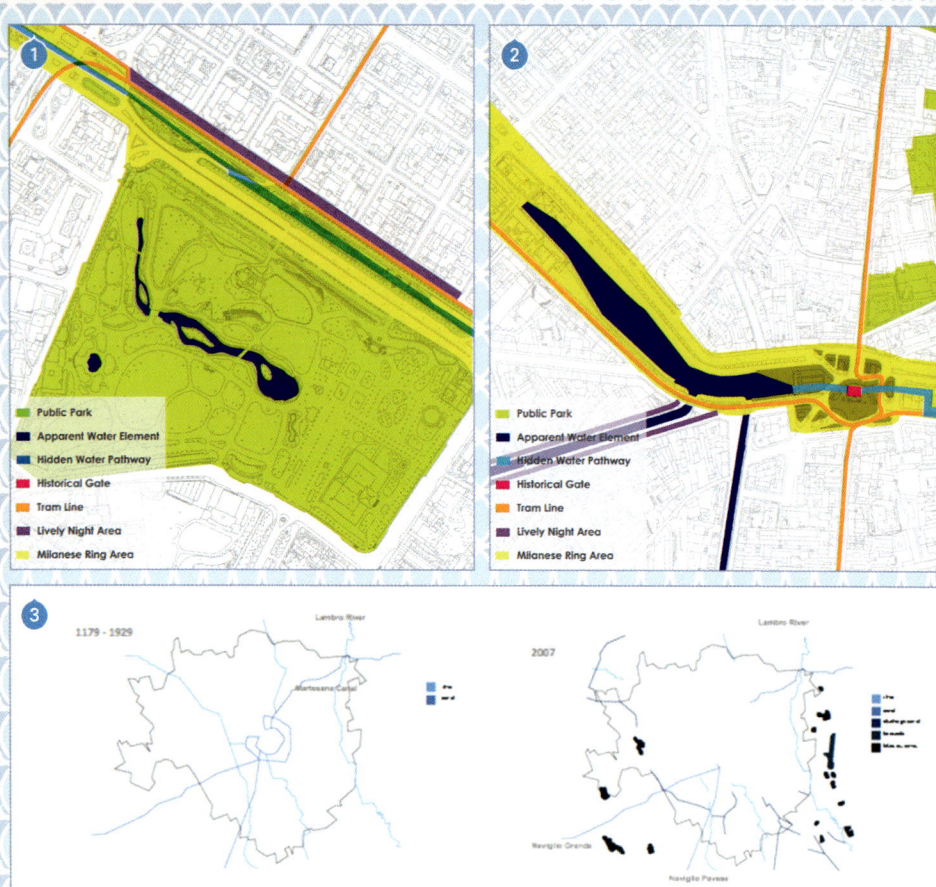

Imgs. 1/2 - Triadic Water Concert, Darsena and Public Garden Indro Montanelli - Hideaki Nishimura
Img. 3 - Situation of the Navigli canals before and after their covering by Karl Maisinger
Img. 4 - Picture of "Chiusa della Conchetta", project studio by Leonardo da Vinci, Milan photo by Gianandrea Barreca
Img. 5 - Picture of "Conca dell'Incoronat"a (or Conca delle Gabelle) project studio by Leonardo da Vinci, Milan photo by Gianandrea Barreca
Img. 6 - Further development. Project title: "Energy flow city" by Hideaki Nishimura, Chien-Sheng Pan - Workshop: Strategies and Visions for a Water City, 2011

CONNECTION

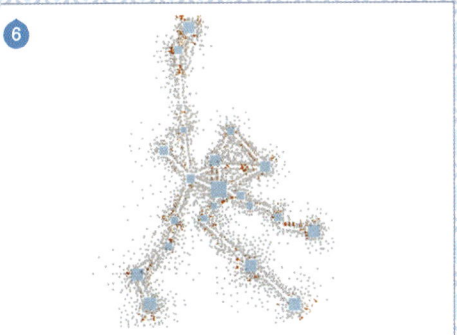

G. BARRECA

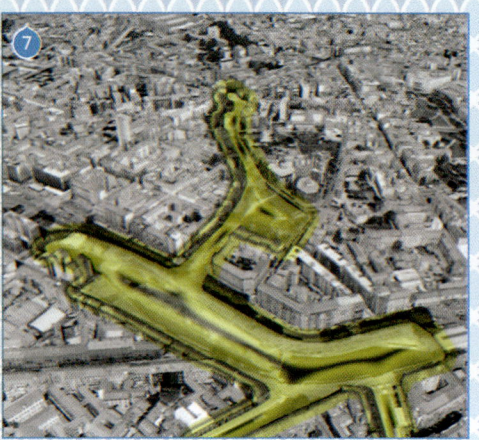
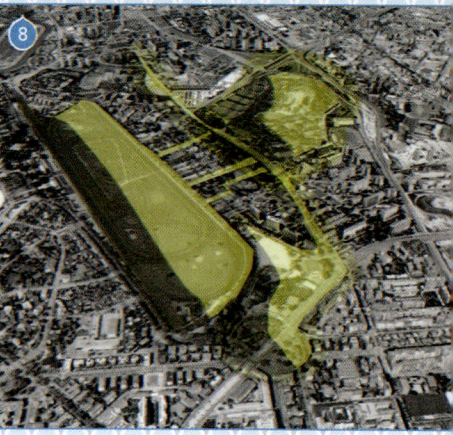
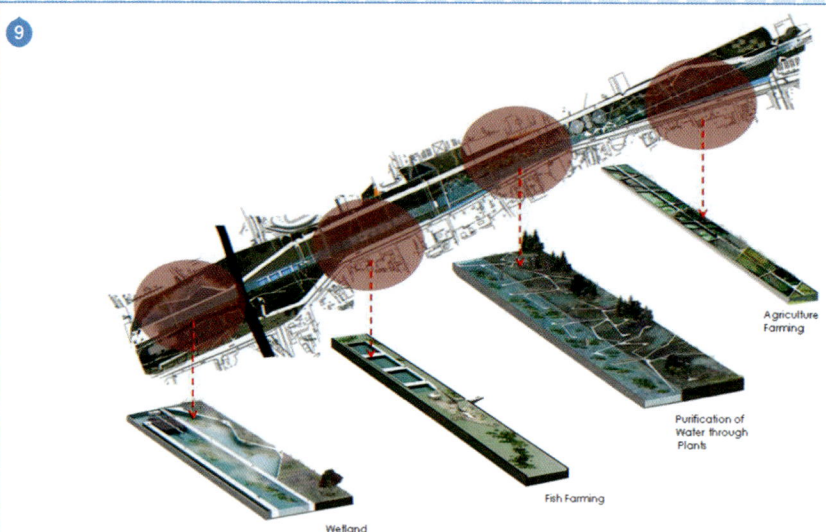

Imgs. 7/8 - Connecting nightlife activity in Milan center. Project title: "Rediscovering Navigli Between history and vision" by Melike Temiz, Final aster Project, 2011.
Img. 9 - Liquid patterns by Sonal Goyal. Project title: "Milan water city, water as element for regenerating complex urban system " - 2011.
Img. 10 - General strategy for medieval ring. Project title: "Behavior of Athmosphere condition" by Melike Temiz, Workshop: Srategies and visions for a water city, 2011.

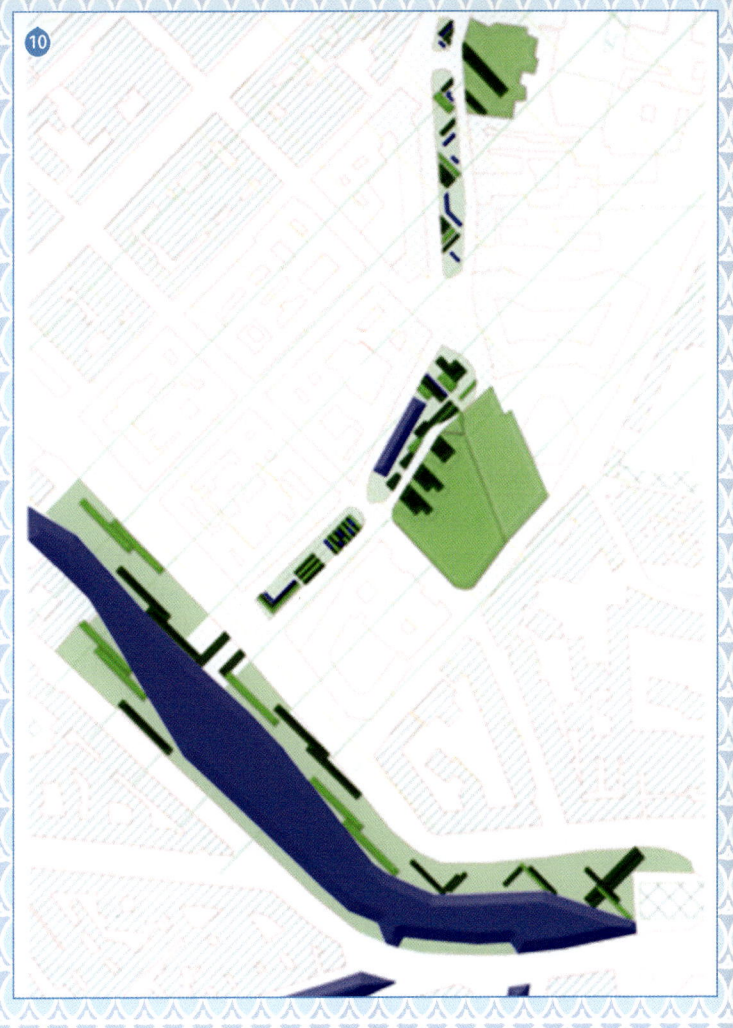

G. BARRECA

ENTERTAINMENT

Aesthetics water

In the history of the architecture of the city, the theme of the presence of water within the urban contest, has always given representation to the borders between artificial and natural in human activities. Architectures of the water brought the representation of these boundaries to the highest aesthetic value. If we think about the complex network of structures and devices built around the necessity of provisioning water to big cities since the antiquity, we immediately realize the deep and significant influences on the aesthetics of the landscape that it implies. Let's examine the case of ancient Rome. It was the city that first gave answers to the need for water within very populated settlements. Romans were the first civilization able to reach the required level of political and cultural complexity necessary to administrate, to engineer and give architectonical interpretation to the relation between natural resources of the territories and a huge metropolitan mass in evolution.

Between 312 BC and 226 AD eleven aqueducts were built in Rome, driving water over a total of 500 km of ducts among canals carved in the rock, lead pipes and the typical ducts over brick arches. Around II century AD Rome had a population of about 1 million and a half citizens, which can count on over 1.1 million cubic meters of water daily provided to the city. Which means a per capita availability almost double than the one of today.

We need to consider at that time a really small number of very privileged persons had water directly provided into their houses. The rest of the population, almost the totality, had access to water within the urban context only through public supply points. The water, once in Rome, was delivered to the different parts of the city through a system of 1300 public fountains, many of which built with monumental purposes, almost 1000 pools, 11 public thermal baths, 2 artificial basins for water shows such as "Naumachia", water battles with real battle ships simulating historical triumphs over foreign seas, and 3 artificial lakes, like the one built by Nero for his Domus Aurea, which would later have been covered by the construction site for the Coliseum.

It is not difficult to imagine the deep impact on the image of the city generated by this massive system of waters and the huge mass of humans and animals moving around it for nutrition purposes, hygiene, work activities, and for public show and entertainment. Emperor Augustus was the first one to build a specific architecture to host water shows in the city. Before, "Naumachias" like the Ceasar one of 46 BC were hosted on artificial basin or lakes, directly dug in the terrain. Augusts "Naumachia", opened in the year 2 AD, was a water stadium long 533 m and wide 355, with an island in the middle and a bridge linking it to the perimeter. A new aqueduct was built only for the purpose to bring water into it: the "Aqua Alsietina" duct was taking water from a lake 33 km distant and in spite of its 190 L per second, 15 days were necessary to fill a basin were more than 30 war ships and 3000 soldiers were exhibiting in front of hundred of thousand spectators. The public provision of water and its devices to supply population and entertain it, shows how in ancient cities the sorts of water and the one of its citizens were stricty related. When in 537 AD the Ostrogoths wanted to invade Rome, they cut off the water supplies to the city by destroying the aqueducts. Thus reducing the higly developed urban society of Rome to a primitive state, forced to bring water from the river Tiber or from small polluted wells. The population crashed from almost 2 millions people down to 40 thousand, the values of the "pre-aqueducts" era more than 800 year earlier. The ducts and arches turned into ruins in the landscape, included into defensive walls or used as quarry for materials.

It took centuries to see Rome reviving the availability of drinkable water from pure springs through the renovation of the ancient ducts and with it the culture of celebrating the arrival of the water into the city through the architecture of monumental fountains and other customs related to water.

In the 14th century, the interest around ancient Rome rose around Italian humanist scholars, which began to rediscover and translate forgotten Roman texts on architecture by Vitruvius, on hydraulics by Hero of Alexandria, and descriptions of Roman gardens and fountains by Pliny the Younger, Pliny the Elder, and Varro.

In Rome, Pope Nicholas V (1397–1455), himself a scholar who commissioned hundreds of translations of ancient Greek classics into Latin, decided to intervene on the architecture of the capital of the Christian world. In 1453, he began to rebuild the "Acqua Vergine", a ruined Roman aqueduct, also with the intention of marking the arrival point of the aqueduct with a "Mostra", a grand commemorative fountain. He commissioned the architect Leon Battista Alberti to build a wall fountain where the Trevi Fountain is now located. This is how the modern history of one of the most renowned fountains in the world starts. The fountain as we know it is the last chapter of a long story crossing the lives of several popes and a quite wide number of architects directly or indirectly involved into the project for a new monumental fountain over three centuries. The final version of the fountain is the result of a competition banned from the Accademia di San Luca, won by Nicolò Salvi. Anyways the layout of the fountain and of the piazza around it is given by several partial intervention after the Alberti's one, given above all by Gian Lorenzo Bernini in 1640 under the pope Urbano VIII. The iconic value of this fountain on the imagination around the monuments of Rome has been very strong. It is one of those monuments who has the power to symbolize an entire city or even a nation.

Those works which finally go on the stamps. It is a perfect example of how the architecture of the water is able to synthesize meanings around a place. Before the first monumental intervention of Alberti, the fountain was just a group of three small basins each on the corner of one of the three streets converging on the site.

The III centuries which occurred to get to the final solution well represent the effort to transform and give shape to a portion of the urban context, and giving symbolic representation to all the powers, economies and values around it. Even with the intervention of four popes, in an era in which they were sovereigns of a kingdom, the works for the new monumental fountain were realized only through the reintroduction of the Gioco del Lotto, a sort of Bingo, in Rome. Strange coincidence if thinking on todays use of the fountain, daily filled with coins by tourists. Anyways, the aura created by the fountain in the place, overtakes its architectonical and sculptural values. Tourist go making pictures to Fontana di Trevi and throw a coin into it, as a fundamental post in their Voyage en Italie. Every year the municipality of Rome raises around 1 million euro by gathering the cents thrown in the water of the fountain.

The aura of this monument and its capability to iconically represent the whole Rome, gave birth to the popular desire to get possession of it, to go over its physical and symbolic boundaries. By throwing a coin to reach its liquid bottom, or getting a bath into it. Like in the famous scene of Fellini's "La dolce Vita". In that scenes, the grace of Anita Ekberg melts its living figure with the sculptural group of the fountain, but above all represents the overcoming of any social boundaries and a victory of freedom and emancipation. Winning over the limits of licit, breaking fragile social rules and inaugurating new times. In the "Tototruffa62", a comedy shot in 1961, the famous italian actor Totò sells the Fontana di Trevi to a tourist, who thinks about the good business of getting rights from any pictures shot to the fountain by other tourists. In that movie of the 60's the chance of selling Italian monuments to foreign investors seems so wierd and absurd to become a cult scene of humor for decades. But actually it anticipated of fifty years the idea that part of the public heritage could be turned into funds by nations and sold to private foreign investors. The last "piratesque" act over the fountain in contemporary chronicle has been the artistic performace by Graziano Cecchini in 2007, in which red color has been thrown on the recycled waters of the fountain, so turned into a bloody liquid in a few seconds. Described by the artist itself as a protest act, it actually, out of the danger of damaging permanently the white marble of statues, is totally an art performance, spectacular rather than revolutionary. Other artists as worked on similar performances, on previous decades, using their work on water to let emerge critical points of view on the boundaries between nature and artifice. The "Green river" art piece by Olafur Eliasson, is an art performance executed by throwing green color into a river, which gets an artificial green wake flowing along the river for miles. Executed the first time in Bremen in 1998, it has been reproduced several other times until the performance in Tokyo in 2001. The work of the danish artist Olafur Eliasson since its beginning is positioned on the ambiguous edge between what is man made and what is a natural phenomenon. Among other works, his art pieces made through water perfectly embody how nature is perceived through a specific phenomenology which can be reproduced and eventually translated into non original locations. Without loosing its effect as "natural" over people turned into "spectators".

Thus in the work "The mediated motion" (2001) in collaboration with the landscape designer Gunther Vögt, a whole floor of the Kunsthaus in Bregenz has been completely turned into a pond with its microscopic superficial vegetation and its mysterious mist, where even the original frozen glass ceiling of the museum turns into a blurry sky that completes the scene. The installation uses the aesthetics of the water element and its complete set of visible features and accessories, to bring the spectator into the experience of really having entered a natural environment. Eliasson with his work makes the spectator his own partner, bringing him to a subliminal agreement where "perception" is "reality". So art brings nature back in public space, and this time challenges the spectators by asking theme to face the borders of their perception and memories. Eliasson methodically visits and photographs complete series of real natural locations throughout the world before reproducing it artificially. Then brings it into cities, public spaces and museums and there he opens the spectators the chance of facing how far they are from their original natural starting point. Eliasson forces the limits of representation, conveying the perception of phenomena as substitution of memories over reality.

"The New York City Waterfalls" (2008) has been an exhibition of four man-made waterfalls of monumental scale at four sites on the shores of the New York waterfront, the most representative of which on the Brooklyn anchorage of the Brooklyn Bridge . Even if conceived on a contemporary idea of "monumental scale", the approach and grandeur of the show in front of the astonished citizenship has been lead exactly as the erection of a fountain as a "Mostra" from the ancient Rome to the late Baroque ones. Advertised as a sustainable ecological event just to avoid the attacks of green obsessed critiques, it is a work of art in the most classical of any artistic attitudes: the challenge into the representation of reality. "Large-scale public art is a part of what makes New York City the cultural center of the world. It excites New Yorkers and encourages visitors from around the world to experience a once-in-a-lifetime moment," said Mayor Bloomberg. "The Waterfalls exhibition is the next chapter in the City's great cultural legacy – and we are exceptionally thrilled that internationally renowned artist Olafur Eliasson has chosen New York City as his latest canvas." Mayor Bloomberg strictly believed in the chance offered to the city of New York and its investors, at the point that the over $15 million dollar project had no city funding and was paid for entirely by private organizations, business and donors. Mayor Bloomberg's company, Bloomberg LP, donated $13.5 million. With estimates that the waterfalls could generate up to $55 million for the local economies.

In any era water art pieces in the public space had offered political powers the chance of publicly show off their potential, and firmly leave a mark in history.

Between 1981 and 1995, during the terms of President François Mitterrand and Culture Minister Jack Lang, and of Mitterrand's bitter political rival, Paris Mayor Jacques Chirac (Mayor from 1977 until 1995), the city experienced a program of monumental fountain building that exceeded that of Napoleon Bonaparte or Louis Philippe. More than one hundred fountains were built in Paris in the 1980s and 1990s, mostly in

the neighborhoods outside the centre of Paris, where there had been few fountains before. Among most representative ones, The Stravinsky Fountain designed by Jean Tinguely and Niki de Saint Phalle; the Fountain of the Pyramid of the Louvre, by I.M. Pei, the Buren Fountain and Les Sphérades fountain by Pol Bury in the Palais-Royal, and the fountains of Parc Andre-Citroen were all built under President Mitterrand and Mayor Chirac. Of course nowadays the use of water in public space is no more related to basic needs as in the ancient times, being substituted by personal water supplies in private locations. This implies the role given to permanent installation of water devices in the cities has been reduced considerably. The spectacular role given by water effects has been thus often related to temporary or special events, such as fairs or world expos. The Expo '70, entitled "Progress and Harmony for Mankind ", was laid out around a master plan designed by Kenzo Tange and Uzo Nishiyama . Two main principles informed the idea of the master plan. The first was the idea that the wisdom of all the peoples of the world would come together in this place and stimulate ideas; the second was that it would be less of an exposition and more of a festival. Over a serial representation of spectacular architectonical events, two water installation were very innovative from the point of view of water shows. The "Nine floating fountains" designed by Isamu Noguchi, which inverted the canonical use of water jets in traditional fountains, were the jets are oriented upwards. In Noguchi installations, iron cube elevated on a pole looked like projected in the air by a series of water jet spraying towards the ground. By hiding the pole with the water, the sensation of astonishing challenge to gravity resulted very spectacular and poetic. The other water installation in the Expo '70 was settled around the Pepsi pavilion. The
japanese artist Fujiko Nakaya created a sculptural artificial fog around the polyhedral dome of the pavilion. The atmospheric installation was realized for the first time, using a system developed by the Californian engineer Thomas Mee, which forced water through nozzles mounted on frames. The result was a subtle vanishing cloud floating around the pavilion, modified by winds and air pressure.
In 2002 architects Diller & Scofidio realized The Blur Building, a media pavilion for Swiss EXPO 2002 at the base of Lake Neuchatel in Yverdon-les-Bains, Switzerland. When they decided their building would have been conceived as a "cloud" suspended over the lake, they asked Fujiko Nakaya to be their consultant. From the architects' description: "The Blur Building is an architecture of atmosphere—a fog mass resulting from natural and manmade forces. Water is pumped from Lake Neuchatel, filtered, and shot as a fine mist through 35,000 high-pressure nozzles. A smart weather system reads the shifting climatic conditions of temperature, humidity, wind speed and direction and regulates water pressure at a variety of zones."
"Water is not only the site and primary material of the building; it is also a culinary pleasure. The public can drink the building." The blur Building by Diller & Scofidio is a work where water helps architecture disappear. The effort is not to create a cloud around a building, but making the cloud a space for itself. Water is not used as an environmental "decoration", but it is suspended into an intermediate state between

ENTERTAINMENT

liquid and solid which is inhabitable. The power of the installation is not only in its contribution to the alteration of the landscape and in its dynamic feedbacks on climatic variations. This architecture has an interior space and its boundaries are not walls nor curtains, but water vapor.

Blur building is an installation about the forced boundaries between what is manmade and what is natural, as in Eliasson work. But this cannot be simply classified as an art work that clearly stands in front of the observer. The user can go inside it and "eat it". This works shows we are in need for new definitions of space and nature. Categories of knowledge evolved into hybrid conditions, mixing what we considered classic, natural, art, architecture. All authors are called to give interpretation and representation to the position of human in front of what is now considerable "nature". It is clear the classic counterposition between city and countryside totally faded. We leave a condition of seamless urban conditions. On one side because of the industrial conditions of nowadays agriculture and its implication on the landscape. On the other side for the new attitude towards the comprehension of what is "natural". A therm, "natural", whose definition is now suspended between neo-romantic "horrible-sublime" dialectics, and a neo-realistic immersive approach. The awareness about the vulnerability of natural resources, is forcing the research of designer on alternative scenarios of "forced/natural/landscape", where a new presence of "live" or "green" elements within urbanscapes is produced through the inversion of ordinary natural layouts, for example between what is vertical and what is horizontal. In this direction the "mures végétales" by the artist Patrick Blanc, have created great enthusiasm between architects and produced monumental installation like in the Caixa Forum in Madrid (with Herzog and de Meuron) and in the Musee du Quai Branly in Paris (with Jean Nouvel). But this direction is not giving an interpretation of the current anthropological and economical situation, where an always wider society is progressively becoming more cultivated and poor at the same time. This makes difficult to think that art and architecture will be called to make urban installation which imply a big waste of natural resources (water for example), but also economical ones in therms of cost of construction and maintenance. In ancient Rome the duct system was turning into urban resources all the available water that was streaming trough the landscape to the sea. Technologies derived from it while new esthetics gave representation to the customs society developed around it.

What is the role of politics and urban developer in a new construction and definition of the territory, is to be defined and reinterpreted. For sure the intervention on both functionality and celebration could find a solution in a new use of water and related architectures. Thus reinventing the contexts of events related to contemporary urban life and its content. In this context, the role of design School is crucial, to give raise to new generation of designers, with a new sensitivity and awareness towards mutated ecological, urban, social and economic scenarios.

The workshop "Water, Art, Ecology", within the Master Urban Management And Architectural Design at Domus Academy between 2010 and 2011, tried to set a point on the chance offered by water into designing new urban devices at the scale of the pavilion, to revitalize desolated urban contests, create new didactic attractions, and experiment living pubic ecosystems. The project "Triadic water concerto", by Hideaki Nishimura, clearly experimented in a contemporary contest, the monumental scale of architecture in the city. The use of architecture out of any functional purpose, in its pure role of celebration, was an attempt to verify the power of architecture to create popular awareness towards the city, its shape and potentiality. The project, in the form of a monumental water duct over arches, was succeeding into seaming the Public Gardens of Milano, with one of the most vibrant districts of the city, now separated by a causeway. The continuos form and logic of the classic language, made visible through the presence of water the link between the two parts of the city. Thus creating a physical and visual connexion which did not need any explanation to get popular appreciation. Architecture then, can still be voted to triumph, even if not celebrating any monarch nor a saint. In this direction a second intervention by the same student was creating a water architecture around the Arco della Pace in Milano, thus making a very interesting monumental intervention around what already was a monument. But that time bringing new urban life over a collapsed triumphal memory of the arch. The workshop exploited the potential of water installation, not only within urban contests.

The chance of creating pavilion for spectacular temporary events, was perfectly realized by the project of H. Nishinura and Chin Sheng Pan called "Water Kaleidoscope". It took its inspiration by the chines Dragon Basins, in which the water inside bronze basins starts making ripples when rubbing the metal surface with the hands.

The architecture created around this simple phenomenon was really spectacular and created and immersive interactive atmosphere. Water while streaming on a lens on top of a conical space, was perturbed by the frequency of the voice of visitors talking, singing or yelling at a microphone situated in the center of the room. An electronic device was turning the sound into vibration in the water. The light passing through the water lens on top of the space, was projecting the live ripples all around the sides and bottom of the conical "cave". Thus giving living shape to the sound. Then the water was continuously flowing down along the external surface of the pavilion, creating a very spectacular effect, but also working as a cooling system for the external surface of the pavilion.

Other works put their emphasis on the role of art installation to show the invisible resources that surrounds us , in spite of an endless waste. Taking its inspiration by the dew gathered on spider webs, Frances Nkese Bassey and Kim Jin Young designed a technological installation in the form of a giant maze of poles covered with a thin web of technical fiber. Able to gather water from atmospherical humidity and convey it into the poles and finally to filters to make it pure and drinkable. Thus providing free drinkable water in the public space. A perfect combination of a urban installation and a public facility.

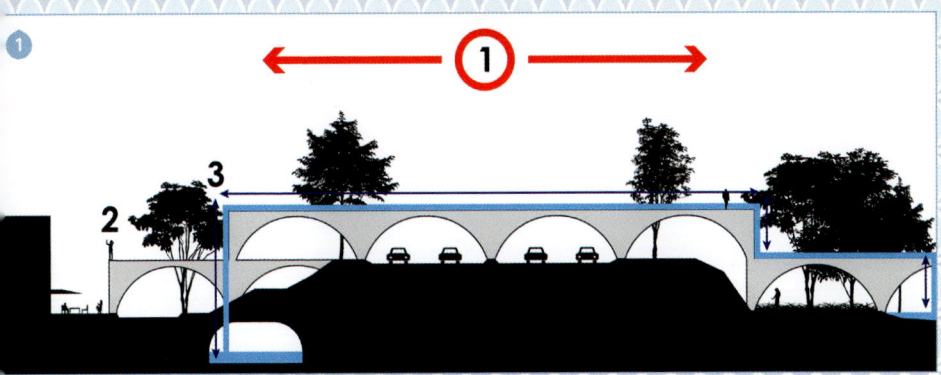

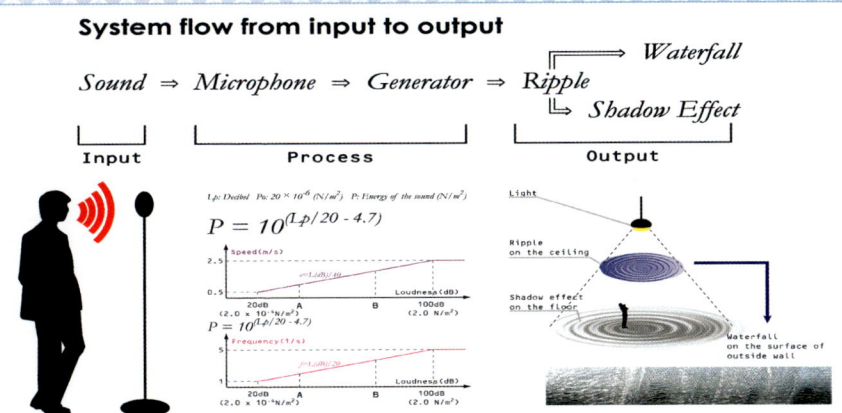

Img. 1 - Promenade aqueduct fr the area Giardini Pubblici Indro Montanelli, design concept.
Image by Hideaki Nishimura from "Triadic water concerto" - Final Master Project 2011.
Img. 2 - Promenade aqueduct fr the area Giardini Pubblici Indro Montanelli, general view.
Image by Hideaki Nishimura from "Triadic water concerto" - Final Master Project 2011.
Img. 3 - Imgage of Piazza Sempione as Multiporpuse Space with water tide system
Image by Hideaki Nishimura from "Triadic water concerto" - Final Master Project 2011.
Img. 4 - Image by Hideaki Nishimura and Chien Sheng Pan from "Water kaleidoscope" - Final Master Project 2011.

F. LIBRIZZI 085

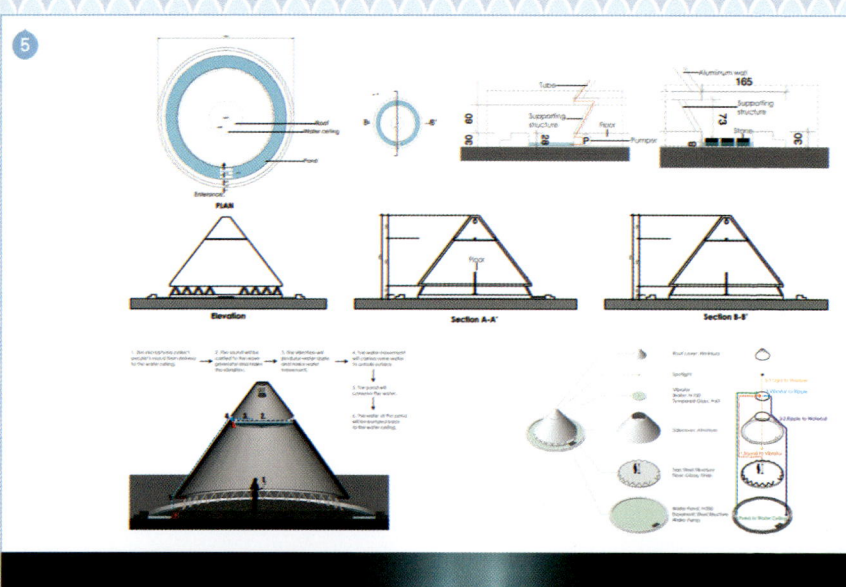

Img. 5 - Elevation, sections and Inside view, concept image.
Image by Hideaki Nishimura and Chien-Sheng Pan from "Water kaleidoscope" - Final Master Project 2011.

ENTERTAINMENT

☐ Water machine as a **single** element within the public space

☐ Water machine as a many components of a single system placed in a **cluster**.

☐ Water machine as a many components of a single system placed **randomly**.

Water machine

1. Social Interaction
2. Aesthetics/ Monumental
3. Environmental Benefits

Img. 6 - **The water machine, interaction with public spaces.**
Image by Frances Nkese Bassey and Jin Young Kim from "Dew webs" - Final Master Project 2010/2011.

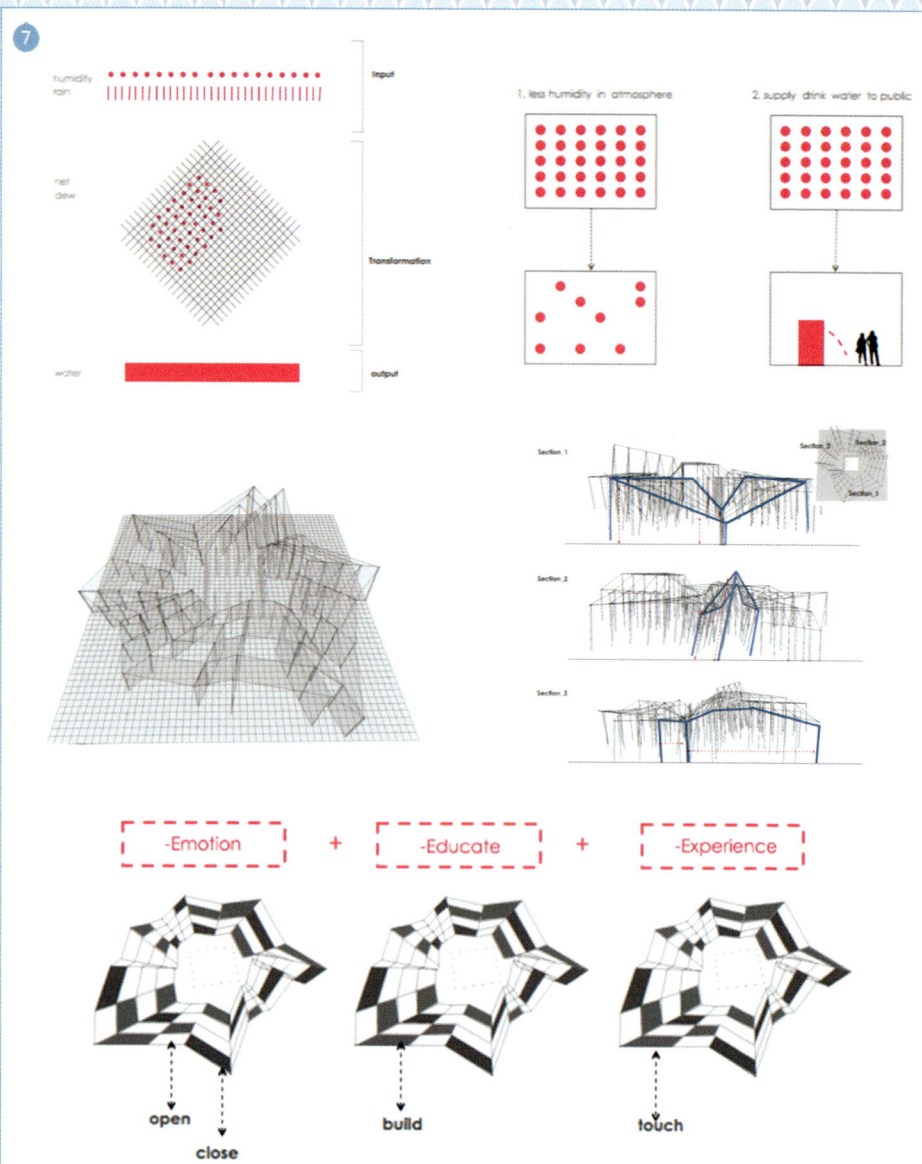

Img. 7 - The water machine, design. Image by Frances Nkese Bassey and Jin Young Kim from "Dew webs" - Final Master Project 2010/2011.

ENTERTAINMENT

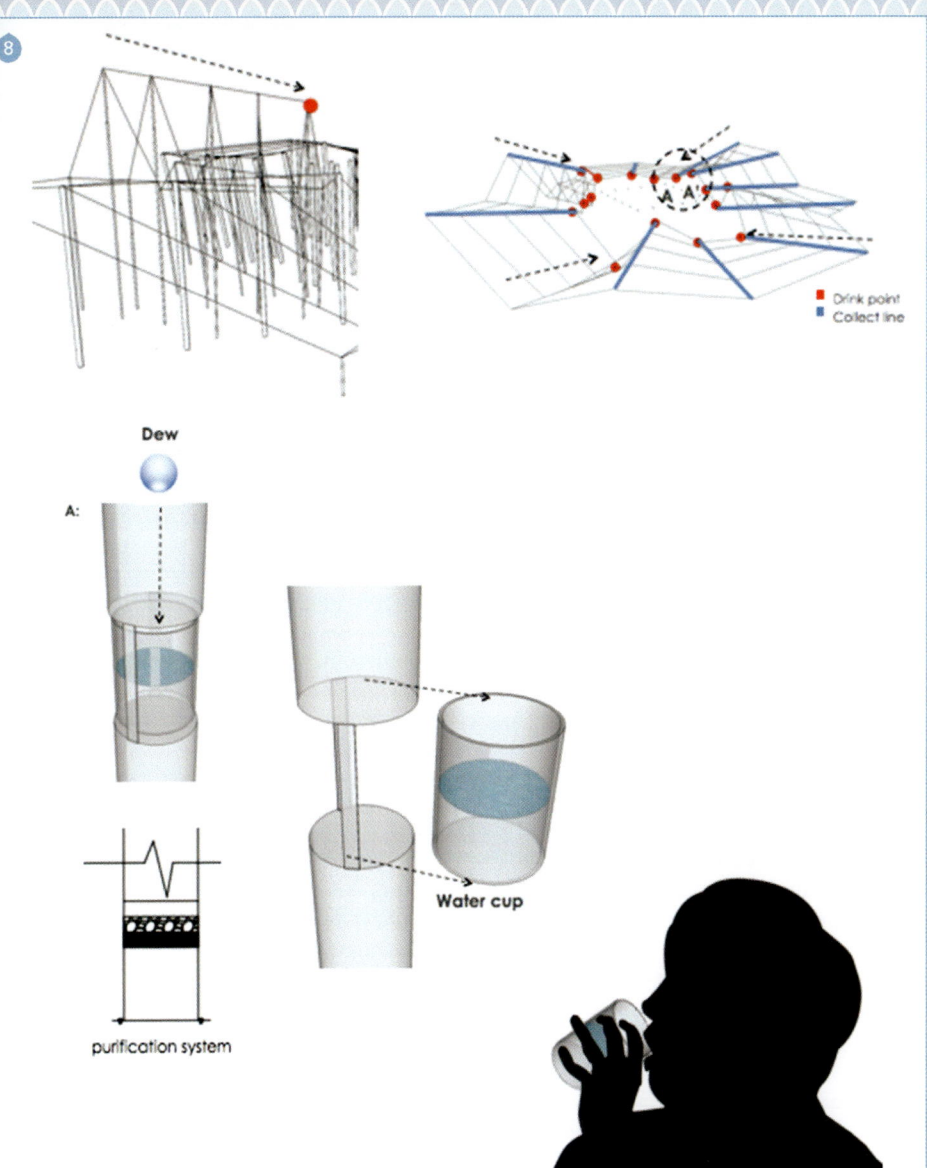

Img. 8 - The water machine, design and system . Image by Frances Nkese Bassey and Jin Young Kim from "Dew webs" - Final Master Project 2010/2011.

Water
A process of cultural sedimentation

Water is the element which characterises life on our planet and which has contributed to the geographical "design" of the land on which we live.
The Po Valley is an example of this: a geographical unit whose existing geological configuration has been formed by the sedimentation of watercourses flowing into the valley from the Alps and the Apennines, forming the great river Po. The millenary water regime has created two completely different geological structures: […] *There is a clear distinction between the two areas, which differ in relation to height, terrain, water regimes and vegetation. The high plain (alta pianura), also called the dry plain (pianura asciutta), lies at the foot of the Prealps and of the foothills of the Apennines; its ground, made from sand and gravel, is permeable and unable to retain rainwater. Water therefore penetrates tens of meters below the surface, until reaching a layer of waterproof material. Water flows along the impermeable rocks until it is able to resurface from the phreatic zone, giving rise to springs or karst springs. These sources, as a result of the constant temperature (between 9 and 12°C) of their waters, have enabled for special water-meadow cultivation techniques to be developed. The low plain (bassa pianura), also called the irrigated plain (pianura irrigua), begins where the line of karst springs begins. The ground in this area is made from finer, impermeable or not very permeable materials, generally clays, which causes water to stagnate, forming marshes and swamps.* […] (wikipedia).
The sedimentation process generated by water arouses greater interest when related to the dynamism of the landscapes created by the same. Water is the amniotic fluid and umbilical cord which enables places to come to life and vegetation to draw the "contours" of landscapes. The Po Valley features rich forests in its wetter areas, the lower plains, and moorlands in the more arid areas, the higher plains. The landscape of the Po valley has been redesigned by a century of farming, during which a network of irrigation canals and navigable waterways were built, making this plain one of the richest and productive lands on the entire planet: a unique and impressive agricultural landscape, where man and nature lived in bucolic harmony.
Over the last century, this "redesigning" process of the Po Valley has abruptly taken off as a result of man's vision of dominion over nature: urban industrialisation has generated an indiscriminate use of water resources, leading to many of the tributaries of the Po (the Lambro, the Seveso, the Molgora…) becoming polluted and resulting in the destruction of typical Po Valley landscapes in favour of industrial settlements and/or land divisions, as described in detail by the geographer Eugenio Turri in his written work Anthropology Landscape. This phenomenon, however, has begun to be confuted by the awareness that humans are part of a broader system: the "planetary

garden" (poetic and wise term coined by Gilles Clement). "Man as a part" and not as a ruler, leads to a necessary reflection that establishes a sense of "limit" to "speculative sedimentation of the land" and depredation of natural resources, in particular water.
In this perspective, the work carried out during the course at Domus by Chien-Sheng Pan, under the guidance of Mason, is a reference to a Leonardo's vision of the unity of water: water understood as chemical element, water as a source of religious and artistic inspiration. Indeed, it should be noted that Mason has passionately researched the theme of water for many years, and his machines are to be understood as "amplifiers of emotions", reminding us that *"it's not time to die"* and that *"all those moments will - NOT - be lost in time, like tears in the rain"* (Blade Runner), but that water is the source of our life and what we are made of.
The five machines designed by J&M bring to mind Jean Tinguely. The machines, nevertheless, stand out by virtue of the desire to create precise geometric shapes, which are more similar to an architectural project capable of transforming certain forgotten areas of Milan's Navigli (system of canals) into "places".
The subsequent mechanisms draw us closer to the banks of the Navigli: to observe and listen to the sound of the water and discover the spatiality of the canal's constructions. The machines are metallic elements that aggregate to form a mechanical, physical and aesthetic equilibrium, able to reawaken memories and images of rudimentary but ingenious mechanical agricultural tools which support and exploit the perpetual dynamics of nature's movement: flowing waters and breezes of air.
Perhaps unconsciously, J&M's study reflects on the history of the Po Valley and provides a recount of hard times: a time in which iron oxidised with nature and wore away as a result of hard work in the fields; it recalls to our minds images of a nation hungry for food and for the future, but which knew how to satisfy its hunger for a few moments by contemplating views of landscapes and was able to relish a slice of watermelon eaten outdoors under the scorching summer sun! (reference to infinite travel by Claudio Magris). It is through this oneiric vision that the machines transform into architectural signs, since they are able to balance portions of existing landscapes, creating dynamic and continuous volumes.
In short, J&M's study instils a process of "cultural sedimentation" directed at the need to perceive water as a constituent part of the city's makeup, inviting us to view and experience water, even in artificial canals of the city, with a more respectful or, simply, more poetic approach.

1. The dangler

A line of metal, attached to a pin anchored to the bottom of the canal and balanced by a complex structure of counterweights, continuously outlines three-dimensional shapes following the water's movement. The rhythmical movements of the machine generate sounds and vibrations of light that transform the bridge's underpass into an animated piazza, amplifying the water's intrinsic vitality.

2. The sway

Along the Naviglio Grande, towards the EXPO site, nature has re-colonised the banks of the canal with pioneer species and weeds. A new form of metal life that flutters like a "lost" dragonfly in a sweltering hot Milanese summer gains shape in the new habitat.

3. The oscillator

The banks made from cement, rising 4 meters in height, form a sound overflow which is exploited to design a machine able to amplify the water's sound. A 10-meter long oscillator, capable of capturing and altering the slow movement of the water in a pneumatic sound, appears to hover in the air like the bow on a violin, generating music that oscillates from romantic and bucolic melodies, to high-pitched and intense sounds of metropolitan life.

4. The vibrator

Pre-existing industrial bridges, trusses, now in disuse, are used to compose a series of machines completely suspended by powerful magnets supporting metal rods of different shapes and weights. The skilful geometrical combination and the rigorous physical study of weights, form metal sculptures which obsequiously stretch out inside Leonardeschi neo-perspective scenery, in which luxuriant nature creates an ethereal and vibrant bed.

5. Metronome

To cross, to go beyond, to wade through, are synonymous verbs invariably related to time, imposing a before and an after. In this work, J&M force actions to cross, go beyond, wade through a line of demarcation between before and after, using a simple metal rod which outlines the central axis of the canal. The drawn line, however, is not a rigid and static connection, but a bridge which continues to oscillate: the parallelism of the canal's banks appears to find the infinite point of intersection and the certainty of a temporal consequentiality appears to vanish for an instant.

Img. 1 - Models of the machines created: spatial signs that come to life through water and generate spatial signs able to create harmonious vibrations of sound, which require a "slowing down of thought", picture by A.Mason.

Img. 2 - **The dangler - Explanation. Project: Sensitive water machine by Chien-Sheng Pan.**
Img. 3 - **The sway- Explanation. Project: Sensitive water machine by Chien-Sheng Pan.**
Img. 4 - **The oscillator- Explanation. Project: Sensitive water machine by Chien-Sheng Pan.**
Img. 5 - **The vibrator- Explanation. Project: Sensitive water machine by Chien-Sheng Pan.**
Img. 6 - **The metronome- Explanation. Project: Sensitive water machine by Chien-Sheng Pan.**

ENTERTAINMENT

D. BERTIN, A. MASON

THERAPY

Open spaces and the water cycle in the scattered urbanization of piedmont Lombardy.
A natural infrastructure project for Central Brianza [25/26]

1. The open space of "clearings" in Central Brianza

Within the scattered urbanization, which now extends almost continuously along the foothill from Turin to Trieste, the area of Central Brianza can easily be identified as one of the most heavily built-up areas. Indeed, the ratio of land cover in this piece of territory is one of the highest in Italy, and the growth rate of urbanised areas has remained high even in recent years, to the point of creating what can now be succinctly identified as a single and congested built-up platform, in which it is impossible to distinguish the boundaries between one municipality and another[27].

Within this extensive and complex urbanisation, where the built-up area is sparser, "clearings" of open space survive, though completely confined within the fragmented and discontinuous built landscape (*Img. 1*). Within these open spaces we can found cultivated fields, flower-growing activities, abandoned agricultural land and natural and wooded areas. These latter are frequently growing in size due to the abandonment of agricultural activities. However, numerous "zero volume" activities (which do not constitute volume, and for this reason succeed in taking advantage of gaps in the planning system, even when no building rights are granted) with a heavy impact on the quality of the landscape are also found, such as vehicle depots and builders' yards, illegal dumps, car wreckers and quarries which are not always regulated. Despite these examples of degradation, these residual spaces are the last remaining areas where it is still possible to see traces of the rural landscape – farmhouses, rural paths, treelines, irrigation ditches – which characterised this territory up to the 1950s,

25. These notes go back over some of the content of a research paper entitled "Per una riforma del sistema degli spazi aperti e degli spazi urbanizzati nella provincia di Monza e della Brianza: il possibile ruolo di un piano d'area in relazione al sistema viabilistico pedemontano e alle relative opere di mitigazione e compensazione ambientale" [Towards reforming open space and urbanised space systems in the provinces of Monza and Brianza: the potential role of an area plan in relation to foothill traffic systems and relevant environment mitigation and compensation works] in which the following participated: Arturo Lanzani, Antonio Longo, Christian Novak, Federico Zanfi, Daniela Gambino, Anna Moro, Eugenio Morello, Emanuele Garda, Andrea Bortolotti (Diap Politecnico di Milano), Andrea Porro, Roberto Spigarolo (Faculty of Agricultural Science) Alessandro Alì, Lara Valtorta Federico Motta (Ubistudio), Gianfranco Becciu, Carlotta Lamera (Diiar, Politecnico di Milano). A partial version of this paper was prese
26. The two authors share all the views put forward in this essay. The drafting of sections 1, 2 and 3 can, however, be attributed to Federico Zanfi, while Andrea Bortolotti contributed to sections 2.1 and 2.2 as well as the images and captions.
27. For specific reflections on this area see Boeri, Lanzani, Marini 1993; Diap-Politecnico di Milano and Provincia di Milano 2006; and especially Lanzani et al. 2013.

and are of great strategic importance in the water cycle and in rebalancing the various ecological systems linked to it, for at least two reasons.

Firstly, these spaces are the only non-urbanized areas situated above an underground geological structure, concentrated in the Central Brianza region, which allows rainwater to filter down through its gravel and sand layers and thus resupply the underground water table, which is exploited about twenty kilometres further south by the collection points of the city of Milan[28] (*Img. 2*).

Secondly, these spaces are the only ones with ground not yet impermeable and connected to the capillary sewerage infrastructure that has innervated most of the foothill urban sprawl, and has gradually reached even the most outward fringes and areas of lower urban density (*Img. 3*).

Today, this extensive and ramified network gives rise to two issues.

The first issue is the very high level of impermeability of the ground. Central Brianza now acts as a large catchment area, which collects rainwater and channels it through the drainage network to a small number of treatment plants, situated alongside the main rivers. These plants are often out of date and in many cases at the limit of their maximum capacity. In periods of particularly high rainfall, they are not able to treat the excessive quantities of drainage water they receive, and they dump it directly – without treating it – into the rivers alongside which they stand. This causes an increase in the levels of pollution in rivers, caused by the bacterial content of the untreated water – in many cases fatal for the fish population – as well as overburdening the capacity of these rivers – which already collect water from the larger basins to the North, along various tributaries – leading to the well known episodes of flooding of the Rivers Lambro and Seveso on the northern outskirts of the city of Milan[29].

The second aspect concerns the extension and ramification of the network, which is sometimes used to serve a fairly modest or even decreasing number of users, and which bears progressively unsustainable maintenance and running costs for the Local Authorities.

28. Moving further west, beyond the basin of the River Seveso and towards the Groane plateau, or further east, beyond the basin of the River Lambro and towards the Vimercatese region, geological structures with superficial clay do not allow rainwater to percolate through the ground layers and this water remains on the surface, within a ramified water system which converges into the main rivers and flows towards the city of Milan, further south.
29. These episodes have become more and more frequent over recent years and involve very high costs for the public purse in order to repair damage.

It is therefore possible to understand the strategic importance of the open space of clearings for the overall hydrological balance of Central Brianza, and the potential infrastructure role that this could play in relation to the water cycle in terms of decongestion of the existing water network and mitigation of the flooding risk.

From this perspective, an urban planning strategy for the clearings cannot limit the definition of their landscape to the vague definition of "park". A rethinking of these spaces from a point of view of the landscape cannot be separated from the role that they may play within a wider ecological function – primarily involving the water cycle – which, as we have seen, concerns a catchment area of citizens much wider than the population of the municipalities in which these areas are situated.

2. A plan for prevention and natural infrastructures

The intervention scenario presented here recognises the strategic role played by these clearings and attempts to be both realistic and ambitious. The elements of realism consist in the recognition and mapping of open space as it really exists today, that is to say fragmented and confined (*Img. 4*), leaving aside the paradigms of the "ecological corridor" and of the "green network", which still guide many regional environmental policies, but which in many cases seem to be forced interpretations that no longer correspond to the real operational possibilities in such a densely and disorderly urbanised territory. The elements of ambition, on the other hand, consist in assigning to these spaces a complex environmental infrastructure role (*Img. 5*), whose functioning is recognised and contained within a concept of ecology that includes urbanisation and the practices involved in it[30].

From this perspective, we can put forward two main approaches of intervention, exemplified by two pilot projects developed for specific areas[31].

2.1 Clearings as integrated projects for public spaces and river water treatment systems

A first approach involves landscape upgrading of the open space of the clearings in which new public spaces for use by the surrounding municipalities are integrated with river water treatment systems.

The area of disused quarries situated between the municipalities of Lentate sul Seveso and Meda, in particular, offers the right conditions for designing a system of basins able to temporarily store and treat the water from the River Seveso, and using

---

30. For more details on this approach, from the wide literature available, see at least Waldheim, 2006; Varnelis, 2009; Bélanger, 2009; Desvigne, 2009; Mostafavi, 2010.

31. For greater detail on the roles of the clearings and on the individual projects see Zanfi and Gambino, 2013.

the surrounding areas as a public park, with grassed and wooded ground, and inserted into a network of footpaths and cycleways (Img. 6).

As regards the water cycle, the advantages to be obtained through this type of intervention would consist in a moderate mitigation of river water flood risks (in this case the water from the River Seveso), as well as mitigation of pollution levels of this water by means of sedimentation and phyto-purification processes[32].

The basins could be organised into a water system in series, within which the river water could sediment and then be reintroduced into the Seveso water system[33].

The same basins could then be designed so as to give a new morphology to the abandoned quarry areas and be integrated into a system of footpaths and public spaces linked to the surrounding countryside and urban areas (Img. 7).

Leaving aside the evaluation of the ability of this intervention to influence the flooding risk – which should rather be interpreted as the need to promote numerous small interventions along the course of the river – we can mention the two main aspects highlighted by this project. Firstly, the interest in promoting integrated landscape upgrading operations, which can produce, side by side, both spaces for public use and natural infrastructures capable of improving the environmental conditions of the areas in which they are situated. Secondly, interest in linking these operations with action to redevelop compromised areas, giving priority to interstitial areas within or on the edge of urbanised zones (such as disused and abandoned quarries), capable of producing enhancing effects also on the surrounding built-up areas.

2.2 Clearings as areas for the absorption of rainwater integrated with a new landscape design

A second approach to intervention foresees experimentation of projects aimed at rebalancing the water cycle in a highly urbanised and congested area, by channelling some of the rainwater collected by buildings towards infiltration into the ground, associating it with more widespread upgrading operations of buildings and redesigning the landscape.

In particular, we explore the possibility of creating a rainwater collection system in already urbanised areas – and in the areas of new building expansion already provided for by regulatory plans – around the spaces of the clearings, with the idea that the clearings themselves can act as large areas for water infiltration.

32. Sedimentation would have the aim of intercepting pollutants carried by the larger sediments in suspension, while phyto-purification would oxidise the organic compounds and absorb some of the inorganic ones and some of the metals carried in solution, or carried with the finer sediments in suspension. See for example Trevisiol 2002.

33. The poor quality of the waters of the Seveso and the presence of pollutants in the surface layers of the land would make it necessary, however, to prevent the water channelled into the basins from infiltrating the ground. The basins should, therefore, be impermeabilised with an adequately thick layer of clay, and, in order to facilitate the treatment processes, it would be appropriate to create a gravel sublayer so as to reduce the depth and allow the growth of aquatic vegetation.

In these areas, the activities of building renovation and demolition-reconstruction carried out by private citizens should be subordinated to the installation of systems for the separate collection of rainwater on the impermeable surfaces of buildings, then channelling this water towards the space of the clearings through a network of connections, channels and landscape works to be gradually put in place by the Local Authorities[34] (*Img. 8*).

The rainwater collected on the roofs of buildings could run through a network of pipes – laid under pavements, integrated with road space upgrading actions – and thus reach the clearings. Here, the infiltration system could essentially be constituted by a drainage basin around the perimeter, a sort of wide "moat" which would temporarily collect water flows during heavy rainfall, and then allow infiltration over a longer time period and, at the same time, which would have a strong landscape value, underlining the entrance to the clearing (*Img. 9*).

From the point of view of implementation, such a system could be put in place in two successive phases. The first phase would concern newly constructed buildings in the expansion areas designated by regulatory plans inside the clearings. In these areas, the construction ex novo of the drainage system for rainwater instead of a traditional drainage system would make it much simpler and cheaper to create the necessary network of pipes and trench sectors (this type of intervention could also serve as a pilot case, in order to better establish the means of construction). The second phase, on the other hand, could concern the modification of already existing buildings and those subject to building conversions (renovation, demolition and reconstruction work) situated within a wider urban area, around the clearings. In this case, constructing the piping system would be more complicated, in particular because it would be conditioned by the presence of other technological networks under the road surface and by the altimetric limitations, due to which the directly interested built-up belt could not extend beyond a depth of 150 metres from the edge of clearing.

3. A different way of approaching urban planning

The two intervention hypotheses described above provide some elements for reflecting in an alternative way to the standard practices that we usually find in the urban planning policies implemented by Local Authorities, particularly in view of the inertia that has characterised urbanisation in Central Brianza over the last few decades. A reflection on the outcomes of this inaction in the medium and long term (Lanzani and Pasqui, 2011) gives rise to at least two considerations.

Firstly, we need to reflect on the effective convenience of a development model in which urbanisation of agricultural land is seen as one of the main channels for

---

34. In designing the structure of this catchment basin, it would be preferable to channel only the water collected from the roofs of buildings to infiltration in the clearings, as this water is generally lacking in significant pollutants. On the other hand, it would be preferable for rain-wash water from impermeable surfaces such as roads, pavements, car parks, forecourts – in particular when polluted by substances originating from road traffic or industrial and workshop activities – to be sent to treatment plants.

producing wealth and for maintaining the overall system[35]. In fact, this model offers greater income and negligible running costs only if observed over a short time span. As it has been argued, the continual erosion of open spaces in already extensively urbanised areas gives rise to a series of distortions, externalities and diseconomies which gradually appear over the medium to long term and which should make many municipalities rethink their urban planning policies. Evidence regards the running costs of infrastructure networks, which are too extensive and in ever growing need of maintenance, the excessive impermeability of the ground, which results in a water infrastructure crisis at times of intensive rainfall, and the lack of nearby open spaces – which is translated into a lower level of social welfare and higher individual mobility costs in search of contact with countryside and nature.

Secondly, we need to question the exclusively expansive dimension still maintained by Italian urban planning today. We have experienced a period of considerable scientific production which has equipped us with technical, procedural and financial instruments aimed at urban redevelopment and at replacement and improvement works to already existing parts of our cities. Indeed, we find ourselves in a situation in which we have rundown parts of cities in need of regeneration, along with an excessive supply of new building which consumes agricultural land and which struggles to find demand, with very negative consequences for the housing market in individual local contexts. In this sense, it is not even rationally economic to continue building on new ground, without having first made the maximum effort to recover and re-evaluate buildings or areas in our towns in need of redevelopment.

Finally, a third consideration should be added on the value of open spaces. They have to be considered not only as beings related to the collective well-being and to the public use of countryside: now they take on a very important infrastructure role, becoming a central element in the more general ecological functioning of the territory, which cannot be ignored by urban planning. The continued management of such a complex equilibrium with sectorial and exclusively technical planning operations (at infrastructural, energetic, hydraulic level) aimed at mitigating emergencies, without establishing deep integrations between these elements and the landscape design, means limiting ourselves to modest operations and, basically, giving up our last chance to affirm certain inescapable principles to the advantage of the habitability of our everyday spaces.

35. Through income for the private sector, and to an ever increasing amount, through taxes imposed on existing buildings and urban planning charges on new buildings for the public sector.

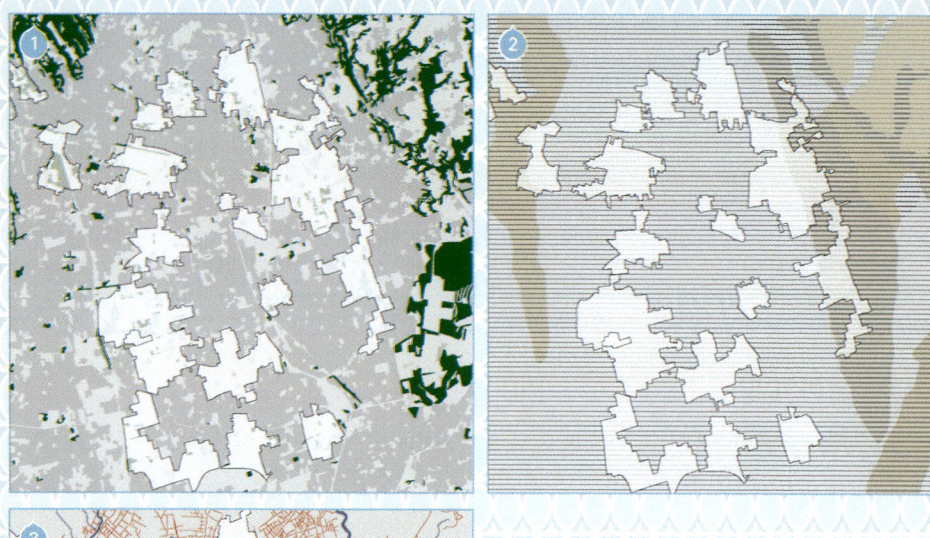

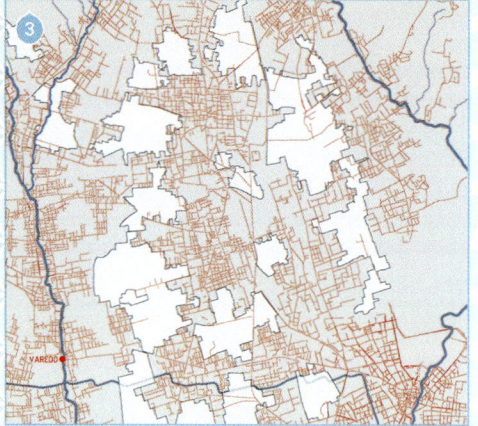

Img. 1 - Urbanised areas and open spaces in Central Brianza in relation to municipality boundaries (sample of 12x12 km). In green the wooded hills of the valley of the River Lambro (on the right) and of the Briantea Moor (top left). Prepared by A. Bortolotti based on data from Lombardy Region Dusaf Database.

Img. 2 - Positioning of the open spaces of the "clearings" in the Central Brianza region in relation to the underground geological structure. The gravel and sand layers that allow rainwater to penetrate to the underground water table can be clearly seen. Prepared by A. Bortolotti on the basis of the Lombardy Region Geological Map.

Img. 3 - Positioning of the open spaces of the "clearings" in the Central Brianza region in relation to the main rivers, the drainage network and the existing treatment plants.
Prepared by A. Bortolotti based on data from the Public Utility Service Website of the Lombardy Region.

Img. 4 - The open spaces of the "clearings" in Central Brianza: morphology and extension. Prepared by D. Gambino.

Img. 5 - The general constituent principle of the project for upgrading the landscape of the clearings:
linear structural elements (slow mobility and tree lines), rural heart, public space
(gateway-parks, wooded grassland, car parks), urbanised external ring within which the sustainable urban drainage systems are to be implemented. Image by D. Gambino.

4

52 ha
64,4 ha
34,5 ha
136,4 ha
220,3 ha
58 ha
91,1ha
201,7 ha
136,8 ha
59,2 ha
477,6 ha
448 ha
61,1ha
252,2 ha
230,9 ha
277 ha
134,4 ha
104,6 ha

5

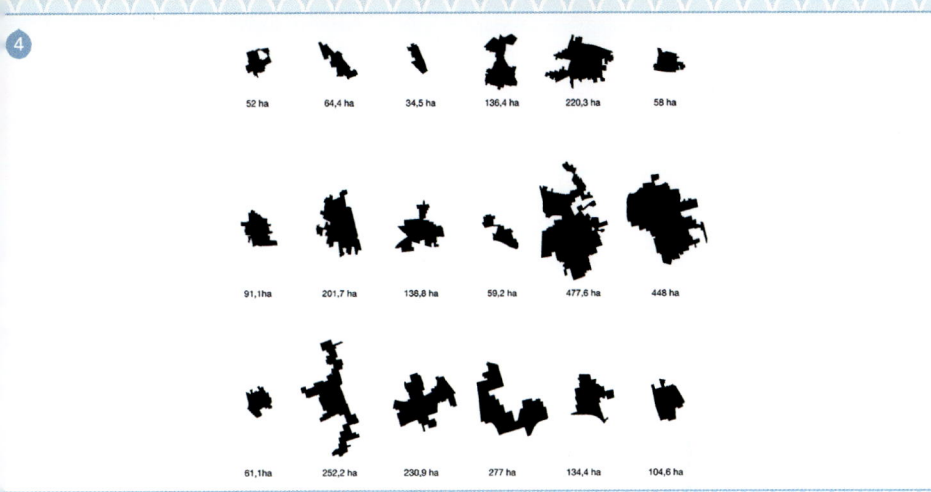

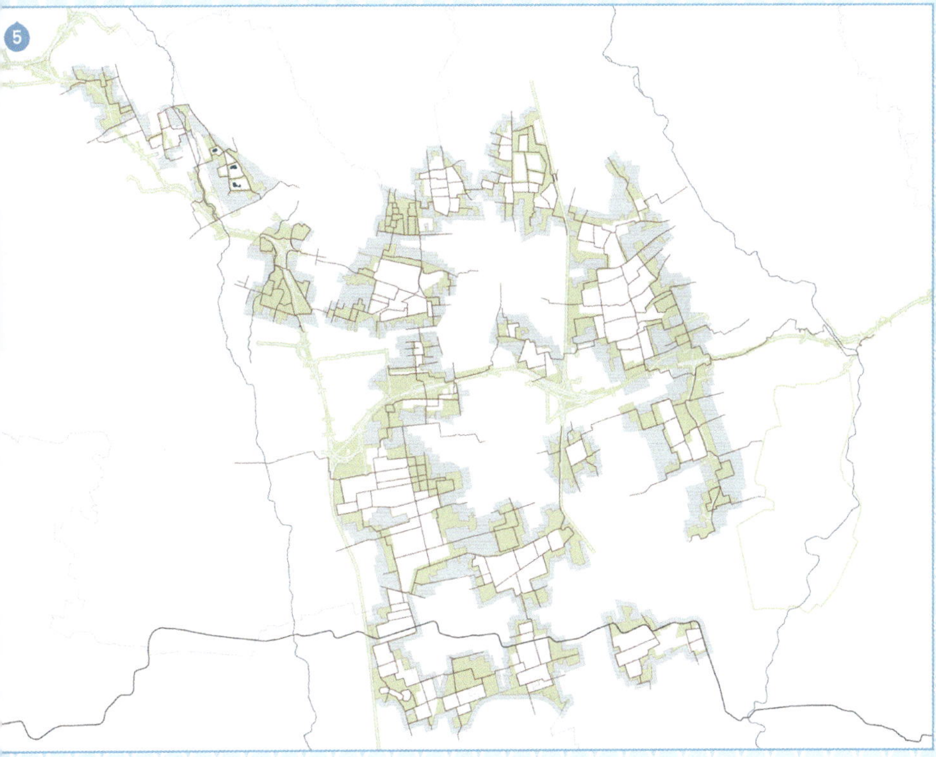

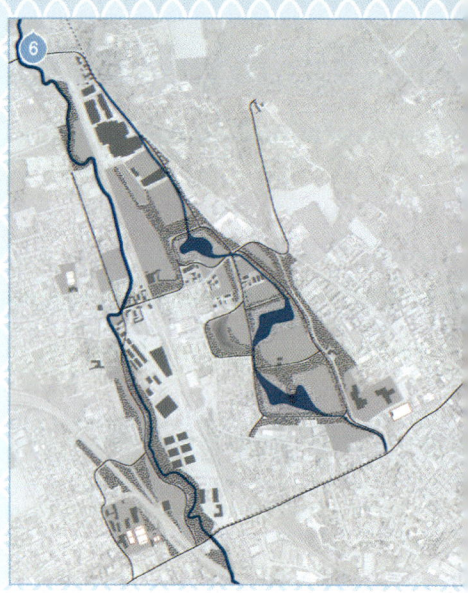

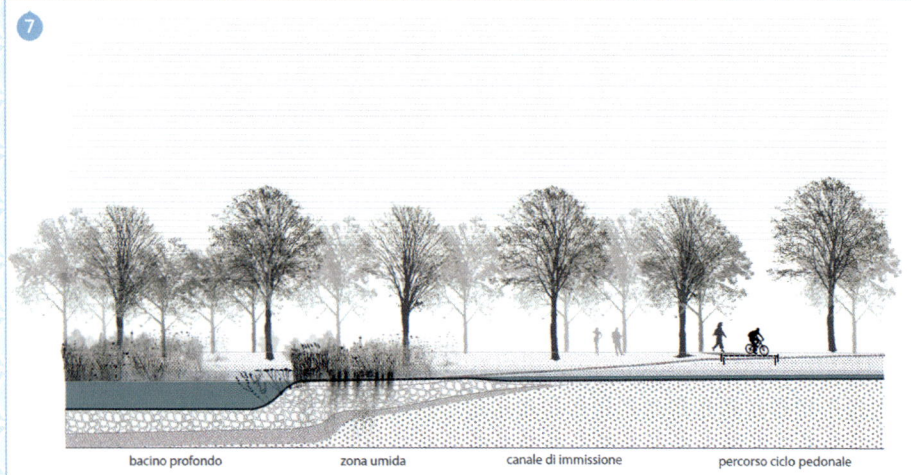

bacino profondo — zona umida — canale di immissione — percorso ciclo pedonale

Img. 6 - **Reuse of the quarries between Lentate sul Seveso and Meda, and reactivation of the Sevesetto irrigation ditch which allows some of the water from the River Seveso to be diverted into the catch basins. The projects offers the opportunity to recreate a final space for the digression and natural treatment of river water, reclaiming the area as a public park. Image by A. Bortolotti.**

Img. 7 - **Sample section of the basins the disposition of the quarries entails partial filling with rocks, impermeabilisation with clay and placement of an ecologically active layer to support aquatic vegetation. Grass parkland and pathways stretch out on the slightly downward sloping sides. Image by A. Bortolotti.**

THERAPY

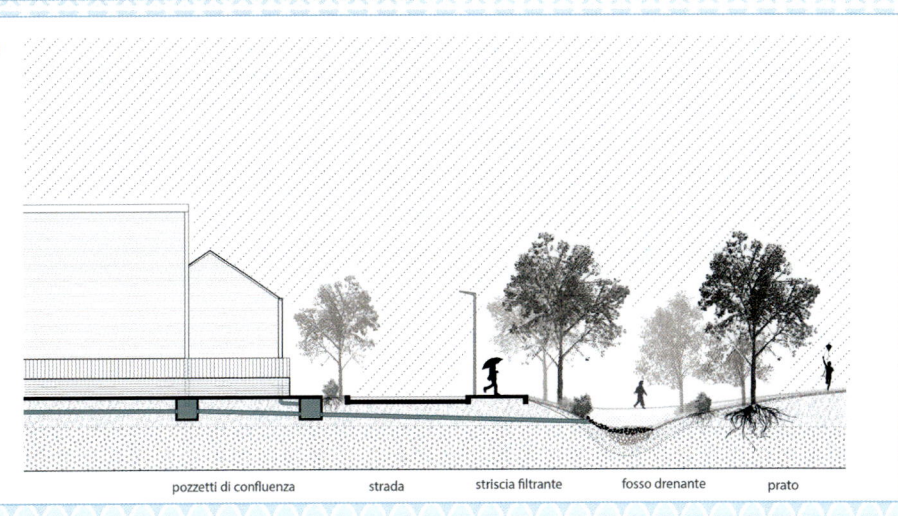

pozzetti di confluenza   strada   striscia filtrante   fosso drenante   prato

Img. 8 - A new network for the collection of rainwater from roofs, connected to a perimeter ditch for catchment and infiltration, is integrated into the design of the open space: apart from offering updating of urban drainage systems, the project provides for the upgrading of the roadway and the edges of the clearing. Image by A. Bortolotti.

Img. 9 - Sample section we notice the connections between the existing boundary road, the infiltration ditch and the green public space provided for by the new landscape arrangements integrated with the drainage system. Image by A. Bortolotti.

Lambro System:
Recovering the water infrastructure

1. Pattern 25. ACCESS TO WATER
"People have a fundamental yearning for great bodies of water. But the very movement of the people toward the water can also destroy the water. (…) When natural bodies of water occur near human settlements, treat them with great respect. Always preserve a belt of common land, immediately beside the water. And allow dense settlements to come right down to the water only at infrequent intervals along the water's edge."[36]

2. Pattern 64. POOLS AND STREAM
"We came from the water; our bodies are largely water; and water plays a fundamental role in our psychology. We need constant access to water, all around us; and we cannot have it without reverence for water in all its forms. But everywhere in cities water is out of reach.(…)Preserve natural pools and streams and allow them to run through the city; make paths for people to walk along them and footbridges to cross them. Let the streams form natural barriers in the city, with traffic crossing them only infrequently on bridges. Whenever possible, collect rainwater in open gutters and allow it flow above ground, along pedestrian paths and in front of houses. In places without natural running water, create fountains in the street."[37]

3. Pattern 104. SITE REPAIR
"Buildings must always be built on those parts of the land which are in the worst condition, not the best. (…)On no account place building in the places which are most beautiful. In fact, do the opposite. Consider the site and it's building as a single living eco-system. Leave those areas that are the most precious, beautiful, comfortable, and healthy as they are, and build new structures in those parts of the site which are least pleasant now."[38]

4. Water bodies inside urbanized territories
We can imagine to follow a Pattern Language[39] methodology to face the item of the recovery of contemporary water bodies. As Christopher Alexander's theory suggests,

---

[36]. Christopher Alexander, Sara Ishikawa, Murray Silverstein, A Pattern Language, ed. Oxford University Press, New York, 1977, pp. 135-138

[37]. Christopher Alexander, Sara Ishikawa, Murray Silverstein, A Pattern Language, ed. Oxford University Press, New York, 1977, pp. 322-327

[38]. Christopher Alexander, Sara Ishikawa, Murray Silverstein, A Pattern Language, ed. Oxford University Press, New York, 1977, pp. 508-512

[39]. Christopher Alexander, Sara Ishikawa, Murray Silverstein, A Pattern Language, ed. Oxford University Press, New York, 1977

THERAPY

we start from the selection of three patterns: "access to water", "pools and stream", "site repair". Their combination helps us on defining a perspective in the contented research and on selecting a series of possible levels of intervention.

Some European cases teach us that only a territorial and integrated approach can be effective in the transformation of so complex systems, where new economical, social and environmental strategies can be tested. We advert, for example, to the German project of the Emscher Park in the Rhur valley, where the industrial heritage has been the start up for the creation of a unique green corridor declined at the territorial scale, dotted by small scale settlements and punctual engines of reforestation, or to the Thames river environmental requalification in London region. Here the treatment of polluted waters has directed a process of regeneration of the natural habitat through the creation of a new wetland area at riverside, equipped by purification devices and able to generate an alternative economical cycle based on biomasses and renewable energies. Milan was traditionally considered as a water city, structured on a diffuse and branched system of canals and basins, arming all the different fields of its economy. The city itself was arising from a complex structure of waters, from the "navigli" organizing the flows and the supplies of the core of the city until the wet basins and the hydraulic nets of the agricultural plain. The image of the city was identified by these spatial devices led by water. The modernity, with its new rules, has superimposed a new logic on this previous order. Roads, industries, residential clusterts have destroyed this ecological equilibrium, separating people from the water bodies, that are now fragmented, inaccessible and polluted, if not completely erased. An anthropological relationship with water, improved in centuries of civilization, is disappeared, remaining only in traces and in the memory of places. The research project started from a news story that has recently light again the attention on the critical situation of the water systems around Milan. The 23rd of February 2010 unknown criminals poured the contents of several silos containing oil and other hydrocarbons into Lambro river, marking one of the worst ecological crisis of the Northern Italy water network. This fact proposed again the main question: how to repair a territorial body totally artificialized and ecologically damaged? Which economical, environmental and social cycle must be activated to regenerate this contexts? Which is a possible mediation infrastructure to determinate a variety of multiscale apparatuses of remediation tactics, implementing a network able to generate a comprehensive development strategy for Lambro river? Are these processes able to create a new water landscape and a contemporary anthropology of living in relation with water?

5. Lambro river. Anthropo-geographical context

The Lambro, left tributary of the Po, is a 130 km long river that crosses in its last segment the urban area of Milan, passing by one of the most densely urbanized territories of Europe. The total amount of population living in Lambro river basin is around 3 million people, including the main centres of Milan and Monza.

The river drains an heavily industrialized area, including productive and technological districts, but also traditional agricultural parcels and a branched infrastructural system. Before the construction of the Nosedo treatment plant in 2002, almost all the sewage from the city of Milan flowed untreated into the river, as well as industrial sewages. Despite the implementation of sewage treatment, overall water quality remained poor, until the disaster of 23rd February 2010: the oil mass (estimated over than 2.5 million liters) followed the entire length of the river, despite both local authorities and civil defense's efforts in order to stop the flow, then reached Po river. This fact caused considerable damages to wildlife and vegetation and its effects will be evident for many years afterwards. Metropolitana Milanese manages the sewer services and the drainage water systems for Milan Municipality, which consist in collecting residential and industrial wastewaters into the large sewer pipeline network until one of the three industrial treatment plants (Peschiera Borromeo, Nosedo and San Rocco), where it is purified for reuse. It also manages the network of culverts of the City's watercourses. About 280.000 mc a year of wastewater originating from the city of Milan flows into the sewage system. The combination of increased population density and intensity of land uses in Lambro basin has put enormous pressure on the canal system; a matter which is added to recurrent flooding events. Also if the residents of Milan are gradually decreasing, the population of neighboring suburban and rural communities is increasing, producing a suburban sprawl subsequent to the deindustrialization process of the last three decades. Residential and commercial settlements expanded into former agricultural areas, hitting the delicate water net supporting traditional plantations. Because of that, engineers and planners have had to design complicated water systems in an attempt to control natural hydrology. During heavy rains it is even possible to reverse water flow of the Lambro river. Despite these engineering efforts, flooding risks and water quality remain a major problem. After the last interventions, the trend is that water is relatively clean when it arrives from upstream mountains and towns and dirty when it leaves.

The contamination is caused primarily because in all Brianza region does not exist any sewage treatment, so sanitary wastes from homes and commercial buildings are directly piped into Lambro river.

The long term contamination of water has also led to the problem of sediment toxicity in the local canals and the river bed. Nevertheless, water remains an indisputable signifier in Lambro landscape. The all territory has been characterized by unique hydrological circumstances: Milan proximity to the Lambro river, as well as its extensive system of irrigation canals, has contributed to agriculture's importance in the history of the city. The main problem today is the accessibility to the water edges, cropped and artificialized by human settlements, also if we can find many parks (Parco Lambro, Parco Forlanini, Cascina Monluè, Parco Santa Giulia), recreational areas, farms and forests in the Lambro region. Many of these areas include connected bicycle and pedestrian paths along the river and its waterways. These common lands and paths are valuable spaces for local populations, a resource to be preserved and enhanced as much as possible. Just as water changes in character through the Lambro region, land uses also vary, even in time. In some portions, for example, industry has progressively replaced agriculture, but today also this model is starting showing elements of suffering. The main result is that sideways uncultivated lands we find the presence of unused industrial properties.

6. A cycle of water depuration

The research started identifying two main lines of action, to be inserted in a general view of the territory: water pollution and the impact of large-scale land uses on the river system. We tried to develop some tools providing a comprehensive understanding of the site and involving the people of Lambro region, who may directly benefits from the outcomes of the enhanced processes. The Lambro river basin can be intended as a regeneration machine, a cycle distributed through remediation nodes solving in different ways the matters related to water purification. The already existing water network will be this way reactivated in a contemporary "waterscape", related to a new way of considering life close to water, the base for a sustainable future for the east part of Milan metropolitan area.

Water pollution is an issue that can perfectly summarize the problems and implications of a territorial approach to urban policies, because the quality of Lambro water reflects the quality and the operation of the all ecological system of the urban regions crossed by the river. Water pollution can have point and non-point main sources. The first ones refer to contaminants that enter a waterway from a single, identifiable source (such as the discharges from a sewage treatment plant, a factory, or a city). Non-point sources pollution refers to diffuse contamination, often caused by the cumulative effect of small amounts of contaminants gathered from a large area. We are talking about the compounds from fertilized agricultural lands, the runoff from streets, parking lots and other impervious areas, which condense heavy metals or suspended solids. Also the interaction between groundwater and surface water is involved, because groundwater aquifers are susceptible to contamination from sources that may not directly affect surface water bodies.

The selection of the areas involved in the project has been leaded in consideration to the treatment scale and the deployment of remediation tactics, but also in conjunction with current and historic land uses, site contamination typologies and locations able to determinate a direct involvement of local communities in the processes of remediation. A crucial concern is also addressed to the impact of the cycle on the

regeneration of sites, which means on the improvement of the environmental quality and on the accessibility of the natural areas. The main areas from where the process of regenartions could start are: the great unused empty green area close to cascina Gobba, the abandoned Maserati area, the parcels surrounding the Idroscalo (fool of dismissed caves), the H shape unused building next to the eastern ring road. Each node works in a second level, after water cleaning, in a social implementation which can help the citizens to benefit from the process of purification and requalification of their area. The case study considered by the project is the segment included between the northern node of Cascina Gobba and the southern one of Melegnano.
As we said, this area becomes a wetland machine, where the income are the polluted waters coming from Brianza and the outcome the precious resource of pure water. In the middle, all the processes of drainage, purification and filtering are translated in architectural forms creating a wet landscape, an original declination of the historical waterscape of Lombardia and the structure for a territorial common land available for the local populations. Architecture translates these phases in an a precise cycle of successive interventions on water quality. The proposed techniques of remediation are: wetland basins and new treatment plants, reforestation and phytoremediation, algae farming and an hydroponic hub. This comprehensive strategy creates a remediation infrastructure addressing the environmental, economic, and social components in a sustainable scenario of repairing.

7. Wetland machine

The cycle begins with a systems of basins in the ex agricultural land around Cascina Gobba, that will allow the drainage of Lambro river waters through large retention ponds. Five phases are needed for the cleaning and filtration of wastewater from heavy metals (like copper, zinc, chlorine, lead and aluminium) and fertilizer: the passing by a pump station, three different treatments and a final disinfection. This course will clean and filtrate the sewer overflow discharge detention prior to release, thanks to the oxygenation and aeration of stagnant Lambro water, and at the same time will provide new portions of water habitat. The enlargement of some nodes will gain surface areas, lowering the rate at which water rises in Lambro river.
Through this it is possible to increase the flooding area of Lambro river, containing extraordinary flood risks and giving more space for water teatments. Wastewater collection pipelines carry the polluted water of houses, industries and fields to pumps stations throughout the area, in turn to transfer water to the treatment wetland plant's pump station. Wastewater treatment enter the head works where it is lifted by giant screw pumps to the top of the preliminary treatment structures. From this point on, it travels through the process by gravity, saving significant energy. Contaminated water passes through bar screens and grid chambers that remove solid settles, that are pumped to anaerobic digesters to be processed into biosolids, then sent offsite to management facilities to be turned into beneficial soil amenities.

Back at the treatment plant, wastewater flows into the aeration basins. Here incoming wastewater is mixed with oxygen and "good bacteria" in a biological process to dissolve and absorb remaining organic matters. Finally filters remove any remaining minute solids and chlorine is added to eliminate remaining traces of harmful bacteria. The chlorine is finally removed from the cleaned water, in order to protect fish and aquatic life, before being released into the Lambro river.

The great quantity of empty lands needed by the treatments includes a great amount of space, creating a real wetland landscape. From the basins, purified water return afterwards into the river, crossing a great part of territory through canals and water pipes. This deployment is intended to be the water structure of a huge recreational area related to the residential and business functions all around, connecting the neighbourhoods with the river. This wetland park will be the first step of a process of connection between the green areas along the river flow, transforming Lambro river in a green corridor crossing the metropolitan area of Milan. This way also the river edges and the concerning natural flooding areas will be renaturalized, permitting the normal life of the river and avoiding the flood risks. The corridor will be served by the existing capillary system of local transportation and connected inside by a net of soft mobility paths, able on attracting more residential facilities, for example condensed in the areas occupied by dismissed or polluting factories. As last consequence, the integration between the different parts of this heterogeneous section of Milan urban area will be constantly improved.

8. Reforestation and phytoremediation

The area of Maserati dismissed factory is the base for the second part of the intervention, concentred on a reforestation by poplar trees and other crops, very good agents of phytoremediation. The huge paved plot of the industrial void will be converted in a unique forest facility, using a traditional plantation which is one of the main actors of the historical agricultural landscape of Northern Italy, the poplar tree.

The artificial areas will be turned in natural surfaces, increasing the possibility of absorbing rainfall and slowing the volume and velocity of water sheet, mitigating heat islands effect due to the asphalt surfaces, creating biomasses and enhancing natural habitats. This area is also in direct contact with some residential districts, that thanks to this will be provided by new accessible green and recreational areas; the future presence of pure water and empty land could also encourage the diffusion of urban horchards and other eco-social practises. Particular plantations and kinds of eco-environmental agriculture could also give in the future new economical opportunities, for example thanks to some goods of bio industry (ecological textiles, biofuels for residential and industrial nearby areas, soft materials for housing, ecc.). Some particular plants are an excellent "mop crop", used to clear impurities, pollutants and other chemical substances from wastewaters. Poplar trees are particularly used to filter sediments and pollutants from ground, surface and irrigation waters.

They can take the form of a plantation or be strategically placed as the final filter at streamside or around a site perimeter. The poplar can also be employed for biomasses yield and harvested for sale as wood and fiber. Additional benefits include erosion prevention, greenhouse gas sequestration and creation of a visual barrier, windbreak and wildlife habitat.

9. Algae farming

The particular topography of the soil, due to the concentration of abandoned caves in the area of Idroscalo, suggests the retention of exceeding water. This condition is perfect to mitigate the flooding problems, but it is also a good contest where to promote algae farming activities. The algae plantations are eco-remedies for decontaminate soil and water, also because they can generate a cycle of organic enrichment processes to restore the organic properties of land. The economical cycle so introduced will create a whole landscape facility, integrated with the surrounding residential and industrial areas basically because algae are excellent biomasses to produce biofuels. The buildings of nearby areas consume a huge amount of energy (in particular diesel fuel for thermal energy), that in the future could be provided by the cooperation between algae farmers and producers of goods derived by algae.

A scenario where polluted waters are cleaned, natural habitat regenerated and new energy production increased, in the optic of an energetic independence of the region. The effort of an architectural view is to integrated algae production in the design of new possible landscapes, where different working models and small scale productions systems, such us micro-farms, are included.

10. Hydroponic hub

The great abandoned building dating 1990 close to the eastern ring road will become the seat of an Hydroponic Hub, dedicated to new plantations and to the final phase of the water filtration (using hydroponic filtration methods it is possible to oxygenate water and to add nutrients to it). The Hub is also intended as the opportunity to create a research centre where promoting awareness campaigns and didactic activities related to ecological items. Also in this case the building renewal interests an area very close to a residential neighbourhood, exactly where the Lambro river crosses Milan urban area. Creating hydroponic plantations, water gardens, points of water treatment and activities directly connected with the river, the idea is to create the condition for an "hydro community".

The aim of re-educating local communities to the cure of water bodies will pass by the preservation of a natural area beside the river and by the involvement of people in a new way of living close to water. The devices of water management and remediation become punctual elements of architectural quality in this area, giving an identity to it to avoid the future abandon and further exploitation. Traditional soil modelling methods, like the bank roads with tree lines, will be used to design the landscape, retrieving an effective method of stopping floods and define fields. All these lines of intervention will recreate an access and direct contact with the river dimension, preserving common lands to future exploitations. The abandoned building, as we said, will be regained as an Hydroponic Hub. The different levels of the existing concrete structure will guest an horizontal cycle of water farms (for plants and fishes) and research laboratories applying the new technologies about aquaculture, fish farming and water pollution. Some specific crops, as we have seen before, are successfully applied for filtering and depuration.

This way the building will be turned into a vertical garden, new landmark off a future water life district, where it will be possible to open an aquarium and commercial or recreational facilities. Also imagine the introduction of permaculture techniques would enforce the new vision of the Lambro river basin in its urbanized segments. Permaculture attempts to closely replicate nature by developing edible ecosystems which closely resemble their wild counterparts. It takes the working connections at use in an ecosystem and uses them as its basis. Organisms from many different biomasses can be brought together for guilds or groups of plants, animals, and micro bacteria which work particularly well together. These systems produce much higher quantities due to an higher availability of nutrients. Its advantages have been proved through practice over a long period and it is the chosen method of water purification in various highly industrialized cities such as London, as well as in many rural communities throughout the world. Finally we propose a water-focused hub, able to revitalize and reinvent the region role as a leader in industrial research and environmentally sustainable development in Milan.

11. Design and management strategies

Which is the role of architecture inside this process of transformation? The scenario we have proposed has all the characteristics of an epochal change in all the aspects of social life and ultimately in the construction of a new life style. Architecture must give shape to this new condition. The remediation infrastructure will be declined in a series of devices composing a new waterscape inside the Milan region. Treatment plants, purifiers, canals of wastewater collection, river edges, flood basins, retrofitted industrial and agricultural areas, infrastructural and water nets will be inserted in a whole frame, the new landscape of Lambro river region.

The complexity of a project of this kind will involve a great variety of investors and stakeholders, in a political mechanism all to be clarified. The proposed scenario is not a masterplan, better a tool to drive the remediation process of the site. The multi-scale system of remediation techniques must be materialized in a network of areas, connections and devices, a remediation infrastructure for the site repairing that will inform all the levels of urban development policies. Probably it would be necessary to create a new dedicated private/public body to manage all the transformation process, including for sure two major stakeholders: the Municipality of Milan and Metropolitana Milanese. Additionally, the redevelopment of Lambro river could be a model for future experiences elsewhere, a catalyst for both an integrated city-wide and a broad regional remediation system. Finally the main objectives off the project are the urban regeneration, the territory maintenance through its preservation, the economical auto-sustainability of the local activities, the involvement of the communities in the policies of transformation and the attraction of investors and later of new populations. Water is the leading item. Because water, inside cities and urban region, is always something different, where new conditions and life styles are hosted and experienced. A perfect declination of the "heterotopia" concept.

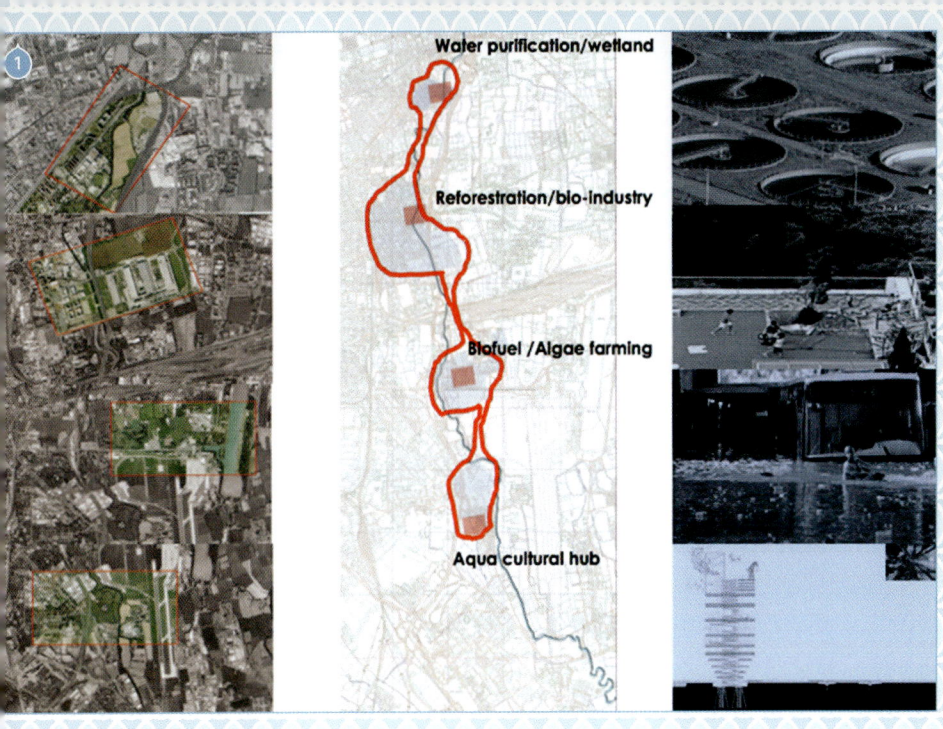

Img. 1 - Remediation infrastructure general scheme. Image by Charbel Attieh from "Remediation Infrasctuture" - Final Master Project 2011.

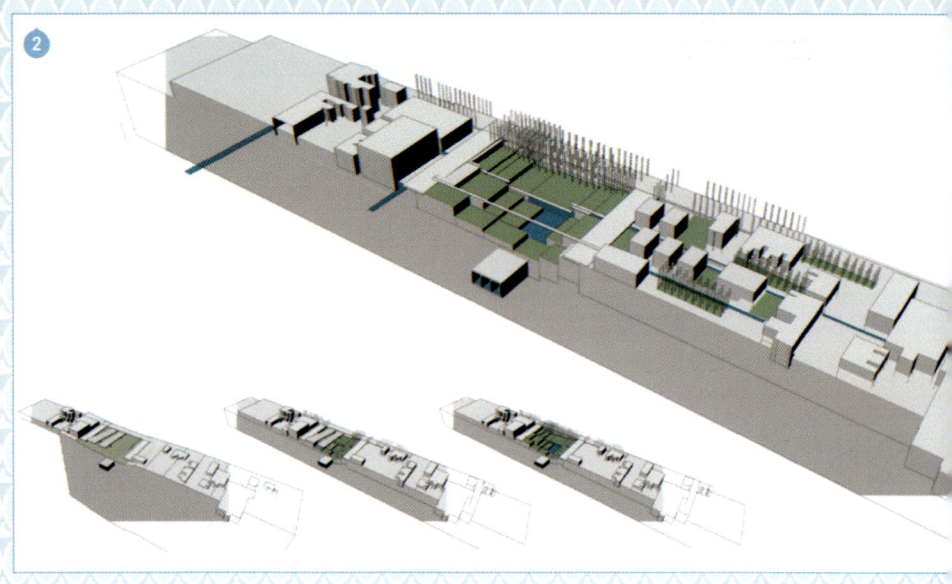

Img. 2 - Rain garden treatment for water management in Lambro river establishing an hydrological matrix through terraced infrastructure. Image by Charbel Attieh from "Remediation Infrascturure" - Final Master Project 2011.
Img. 3 - Lambro river basin: remediation tactics and design strategies. Image by Charbel Attieh from "Remediation Infrascturure" - Final Master Project 2011.
Img. 4 - Main historical phases of Milan water-net.. Image by Frances Nkese Bassey from "Dynamic Fluidity" - Final Master Project 2011.

THERAPY

Territorial & Urban requalification project
Lambro river : DESIGN STRATEGIES

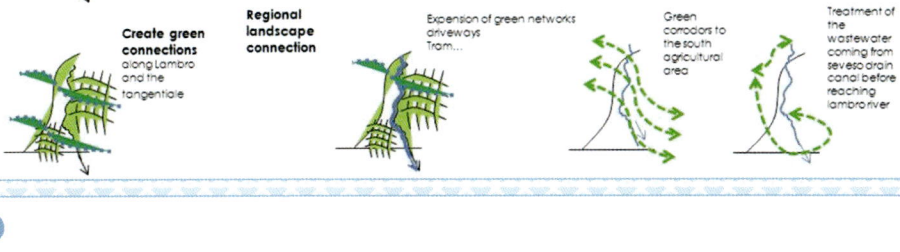

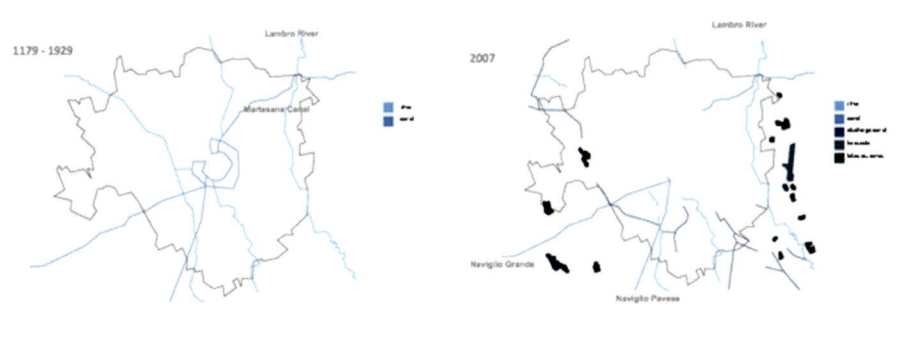

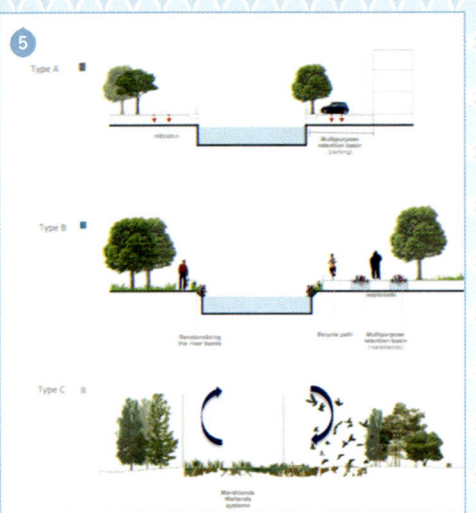
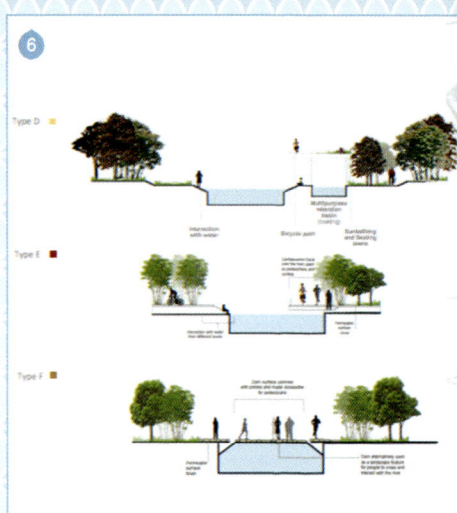
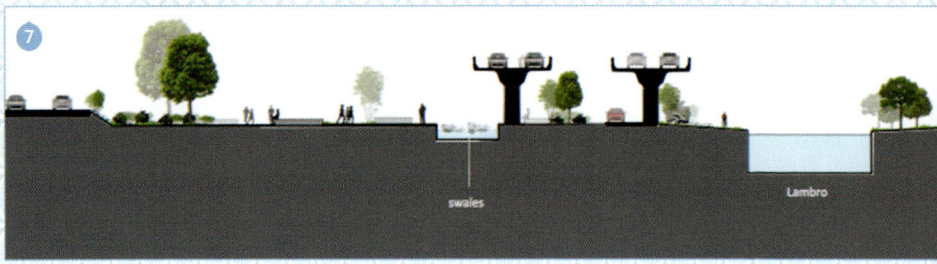

Img. 5 - Scenario: riverside remediation interventions. Image by Frances Nkese Bassey from "Dynamic Fluidity" - Final Master Project 2011.
Img. 6 - Scenario: riverside remediation interventions. Image by Frances Nkese Bassey from "Dynamic Fluidity" - Final Master Project 2011.
Img. 7 - Scenario: remediation of the intersection between an infrastructural axis and a riverside renaturalized area. Image by Frances Nkese Bassey from "Dynamic Fluidity" - Final Master Project 2011.
Img. 8 - Scenario: waterscape of a retention basin. Image by Frances Nkese Bassey from "Dynamic Fluidity" - Final Master Project 2011.

Urban growth in the river valley:
the Italian experience and the doctor analogy

Introduction

Since from ancient time water has been the attraction for the human settlement, most of the oldest and important cities in the word were built along the valley course of rivers. For centuries these areas were selected by anthropic settlement not only due to their easy access to the water for drinkable, irrigation and energy production, but also for the easy urbanisation settlement due to the absence of topographic constrains. Nowadays in the urbanization processes the technologic development of the last decades has in some way compensated the advantages of the vicinity to the water, but the absence of topographic constrains in the river valley is still, in the web era, the most valuable attractive characteristic for human settlement and his economic activities . This is evident in a recent time observing the growth of large urban settlement in the river valley area. The easy land use for anthropic settlement together with a high demand of space for residential and commercial building constructions has determined a large use of the land in the river valley most of time without paying proper attention to the river or creek courses, to their hydrologic flow regimes as well as to their geomorphologic patterns (Leopold et al., 1995).
This attention seems, in the recent time, to be dampened especially for those new urbanised area in the valleys of small creeks characterized by high variability of discharge. This is mainly due to the combination of two main issues: the low value of the ordinary discharges of small river basin, especially in semi arid and arid climate where the river bed is dry for most of the time; people's lack of river perception.

River stream: both a static and dynamic fluid

Fluid definition is often underlined in the urbanisation processes of valley river areas when new space needs to be subtracted from the river flood plain. It is often assumed that the river flow can be delimited by banks, in an artificial water course determined by urbanisation requirement rather than by the physics of a stream flow. Behind this approach there is and there was the erroneous identification of river flow with a static fluid: an element that due to the absence of its shear resistance, assumes the shape of the recipient in which it is contained. This assumption ignores or neglects the concept of mass and energy and their variation in time, that on the other hand characterize the river flow as a result of interrelated hydrologic, hydraulic and geomorphologic processes. Several designs of hydraulic works have been and are made to support urbanisation growth based on these hypotheses, relying furthermore on the fact that generally the positive effects of river hydraulics cannot be perceived over a short period of time, due to the relative low frequency of the design peak discharges. The result of this assumption, made by politics, city administrators and technical people under the pressure of land need, is often evident by observing the new assessment of flood plains where rivers are confined in artificial courses with narrow sections and bends which, on the paper, justify the growth of the city modern quarters. It is not a case, that observing the urban areas of many cities, the ancient settlements were often located in positions that were safer from the dangers of flooding compared to modern ones. The past experiences of people living in flood areas and those in charge of governing cities also appear to be in conflict with the previous assumption. The memories of floods are generally short lived, due to the fact that flood risk mitigation actions are mainly in conflict with the use of the territory, but also because people's lives are characterised by other impellent activities. People demand emergency actions immediately after floods and those in charge are blamed and attributed responsibility for not taking action. However, those demanding action soon become the opponents of the same, due to the consequent limitations imposed on land use.

Flood hazard and Hydrogeologic risks

The erroneous consideration of the physic of the river flowing through an urban area, together with the bad maintenance of its cross sections is often one of the main causes of inundation during floods resulting in spiralling damage costs following the increasing value of activities located in urbanised valley areas. By examining the inundation maps of most Italian rivers drawn up over the past decades and recent inundation events it can be argued that flood hazard is often heightened by urbanisation pressure rather than by natural phenomena. This can be seen more frequently with regards to small creeks where discharge regime is highly variable and closed correlated to rainfall intensity fluctuations. The image 1 reports the cases determining inundation of a semi arid river basins. It is shown that the insufficient size of the bridge river section respect to design discharges is the primary cause of inundation (Dovera, et al., 2000, Mancini and Valsecchi, 2007).

Hydraulic risk mitigation

Italian and European government have recently drawn up formal directives to quantify and map the flood risk on the territories crossed by rivers and creeks (The European Flood Directive 2007 /60 EC , Italian Low 267/98). The "Flood Directive" sets out common lines of activity, in part already operative, in several countries of the European Union, which require study and planning at basin scale, mapping of flood hazard and risk areas along river valleys and highlight the need of flood risk management plans. The concept of risk and hazard are well established today not only in the scientific community, but also among operative urban planners and among city authorities. In fact since the 1998 the Italian Government (Italian Low 297/98) followed by the European Union (Directive 2007/60) defined regulations to identify and mapping hazards and inundation risks along the main river valleys. River basin authorities are now required to edit Hydrogeologic Risk Assessment Plan on a technical scale of about 1:10'000 (called Hydrogeologic Master Plan , PAI in Italy) for any river basin, mapping inundation risk areas and the actions to mitigate the inundation risk trough potential future hydraulic works and safety measures. The latter are the main strength of the plan since they govern what are the possible activities in the risky areas in accordance with the degree of actual risk, irrespectively of any defined urban development plans.

Risk or the expected damage for a given area is defined from the expression:
$R = H_i * E * V$
where: H_i is the flood inundation hazard, caused by the flood discharge routing in the river sections, that occurs at a given frequency with river hydraulic of river stream; E is the type of construction present in the valley area such as buildings, infrastructures, productive plants and V is the degree of loss or damage of each construction caused by the flood stream. The risk R therefore assumes the form of a-dimensional index between zero and one if all the factor are expressed as a-dimensional values or the dimension of a currency if, E, is expressed in terms of element value (Munich re et al., 2011). This become questionable when in addition to the element values, E, the possible loss of human life in the hazard areas can occur during a flood event.

This equation expressing the risk and its application to the territory it is not as simple as may first appear. Moreover the equation should be as result of three main interrelated considerations: (i) economic and politic impacts produced on the territory, (ii) the technical spatial scale at which it is applied; (iii) and last but not least the scientific and technical knowledge required to use the same correctly (Maidment, 1993, FEMA, 2002, Ravazzani et al , 2009, 2013). Frequently the undertaken of one of these considerations has generated, during the editing processes of the plan, a big lost of time and resources increasing some time the risk areas. Image 2 shows an example of inundation areas for the design discharge of 200 years "return period" or at a frequency of 0,005. Flood risk maps should not be envisaged, as often occurs, as a merely list of dangerous areas, which are then governed by very restrictive urbanisation and land use regulations leading to loss of economic value (Hall and Penning-Rowsell, 2011). In fact, this conception produces a strong aversion to the Plan by the same people living in the dangerous areas, which is reinforced by local authorities, against river basin authorities, leading to amendments made to final risk plans taking a long time. This leaves space for discussion under the consultation framework, which most of time are not based on the laws of physics, while at the same time producing a lack of regulations which speed up urbanisation activities limited or prohibited by the plans. It is like taking a picture of a moving target and spending an incommensurable amount of time, with respect to the movement of the target, in developing the film. Will that picture still be useful?

Currently, the time required to take a decision on these issues is often too long and probably the noble idea of participation, highlighted in the Water Framework Directive (2000), should be supported by actors with a greater degree of the phiscal processes involved rather than from the interest of lobbying.

Climate change and flood risks

A recent and on-going debate is that of whether climate changes can increase flood hazards, due to potential increases in peak river discharges at a given frequency of occurrence. Flood frequency under different climatic conditions has been analysed in several international research projects, in which peak discharges are simulated using numerical hydrological models employing meteorological inputs computed from climate models to simulate scenarios of the near future (ACQWA, 2013).

This topic is still open to scientific debate: no "stationary statistics", lack of significant data and climate model simulation reliability all contribute to heating up scientific and politic debate. Nevertheless, it cannot be ignored that climate change, due to natural or anthropic forces, contributes to increasing the uncertainty of design variables of those hydraulic systems designed to regulate the use of water resources. An example of this is the design of river hydraulic sections for risk mitigation or new urban plan development where accurate analysis should support design. This attention and more accurate analysis is also requested in the last European Floods Directive (2007). The effects of climate change on river discharges is not the only cause of increasing flood hazard in urbanised areas. In fact, the absence of river cross section maintenance and river cross section width reduction, may have similar or bigger effect on water levels and consequently on inundation hazard, determine by a discharge increase from potential climate change processes. Therefore the effects of climate change need to be considered when working out solutions as a possible source of uncertainty and should be taken into consideration during the design stage. It follows that greater attention needs to be paid today, respect to the past, when designing river cross section geometry and relevant hydraulic structures, rather than hiding problems waiting for scientific responses to potential climatic change effects.

Structural and non-structural hydraulic defence

Risk maps and the relative plans should be used as decision support tools for risk mitigation and should be seen as an opportunity to improve the use of territory under sustainable risk, helping the river basin authority to define the type of mitigation actions splitting the available economic resources between the structural hydraulic works and non-structural defence systems. This exercise is and was well known in the engineering schools where the design of the hydraulic structures is indicated as the "optimal solution", balancing the cost of the works and the risk mitigation.

This choice needs a good knowledge of the physical and environmental processes involved in the river stream as well as the knowledge of the implications of the urbanisation process of new or old areas. In both cases hydraulic risk mitigation actions whether structural or non structural actions, needs to be closely connected with urban planning of new or existing urban area. Any mitigation risk activity have to be considered not as an impediment to urbanisation development as is conceived most of time, but as an opportunity to improve urban environments.

The following illustrates an important approved design of urban area structural works (2010), which resolves hydraulic flood risks, while at same time receiving important feedback on urbanisation. The design was supported by local town authorities and by the River basin authority of Region of Liguria. The design consists in enlarging the river sections of an urbanised river situated in the town of Vallecrosia (Imperia, Italy) with the object of drastically reducing existing hydraulic risks, while simultaneously improving connections between the centre of Vallecrosia and its sea water front, which had been interrupted since the 1930 by the international railway embankment. The current situation presents a largely undersized river section whose final section is also artificially covered by a parking area (*Img. 3*).

The designed solution, briefly reported in the following Image 4 and Image 5, presents: (i) an enlargement of the existing river section from the actual width of 15 m to 23 m, (ii) the modification of the actual section lead in a larger one of 23 m width at the same elevation, (iii) rectification of the existing artificial curve at the river mouth, (iv) a construction of a new bridge along the rail way. In addition the project considers also the delocalisation of two buildings that are currently built on the river bank constraining the river width to an actual width of 15 meters.

Nowadays, the costs of structural hydraulic works not only include direct costs relating to hydraulic defence structures designed in accordance with peak discharge values, but also includes the costs of maintaining the designed structures. The cost of maintenance is determined by daily interactions of the river stream with the designed hydraulic works. Evaluation of which requires knowledge and quantification of the physical processes involved. Without constant maintenance activities, there is the risk that very expensive hydraulic works will malfunction when their functionality is required. Often, the works committed immediately after flood events are designed only for peak flood discharge, an event that occurs extremely infrequently, without considering the effect of the same works on daily river flow. For these reasons, contrary to public opinion, large river hydraulics solutions are not always the safest of solutions. River hydraulic process simulations, especially river bed evolutions caused by the river bed solid transport and vegetation growth have to be considered to quantify the frequency of maintenance activities and consequently to the identifying the right solution. In addition to structural hydraulic defence works, the demolition of improperly built structures in the river flood sections should be considered. Defence of any such structures may obtained with structural costs that are often greater that the property to be defended and also with several constrains on hydraulic processes and on territory management. This approach, which should be intuitive, is frequently opposed by the population and local authorities residing in the dangerous areas, despite this concept being very well emphasised in Italian law since 1998 (Italian Legislative Decree 267/98). Image 6 reports an example of a house demolition and the enlarging of a historical bridge after serious flooding occurred in 1992 of the Quiliano river in the Liguria region. The project idea was implemented in 1995 and is one of a few examples in Italy in this field. It was supported at that time by the Province of Savona and the municipality of Quiliano town.

A non-structural approach, on the other hand, does not reduce the hazard as the structural defences does, but mitigates the flood risk trough the reduction of the vulnerability of the elements exposed to the flood (V in the risk equation) using safety measures that have to be activated when the dangerous flood event is forecasted (Penning-Rowsell et al. , 2002)

The application of this type of approach requires three main ingredients: a robust flood forecast model, a civil protection plan that specifically considers the dynamics of potential inundations of different magnitudes, and a operative local structure.

Today, flood forecasting experience has made interesting and useful progress, integrating meteorological forecast models and distributed hydrologic hydraulic models (Ravazzani et al.,2007, Rabuffetti et al 2008, Ceppi et al , 2010).

These approach allows to predict with a time "forecast horizon" of 24 to 48 hours the occurrence of dangerous flood with a given probability of occurrence, allowing for site specific safety measures previously identified in the Civil Protection Plan. The following figures illustrate two types of flood forecasting systems: (i) the warning system based on rainfall thresholds computed for a given river cross-section, implemented for the Arno river basin Authority in Florence (*Img. 7*) and (ii) the flood forecast for the Seveso River in Milan based on the computation of the entire forecasted flood hydrograph (*Img. 8-9*).

Concluding Remarks and the doctor analogy

Single conclusions on rivers and urbanisation can lead to underestimations of problems. To avoid the reproduction of past errors in new development areas, rivers and urbanisation processes should be viewed as one problem, identifying solutions so that population and their activities are able to cope with a sustainable flood risk.

The identification of a specific solution should be viewed by technical operators and authorities in the same way that a medical doctor defines the patient therapy. When a doctor visits a patient first he identifies the problem ad the patient's general condition, than he prescribes the analysis to be conducted. Further to this, supported by analysis results, the doctor provides his diagnose and defines the specific therapy. In the same way that good doctor prescribes therapy, backed by test results, technical operators and administrators should identify solutions in a urbanised river valley with the support of processes analysis. In order to quantify the design variables and to identify relevant solutions the processes analysis has to be fully understood, especially in those area where these processes present high variability, as in the arid and semi arid climates. In this respect, urbanisation plans should consider knowledge of the physical process involved and their honest quantification. At the same time, however, engineering hydraulic solutions should be identified also with the idea of improving town urbanisation, reducing as far as possible their impact on environmental processes and human activities.

Generally the benefits of hydraulic structures are verified over a period of decades (flood frequencies), while urban infrastructures exert their action daily. Hydraulic works need to be designed not only in accordance with maximum hydrologic hydraulic loads, but also in accordance with those environmental processes that interact on a daily basis with the structures. This is similar to a medical therapy for specific disease, where the medicines used to solve problem should not cause new problems for patients.

Probably, especially in already urbanised areas, the solution lies in the combination of structural and non-structural works.

The analogy with doctors helps us to remember that hydraulic problems in urban areas, seems similar to health problems, that cannot be solved with predetermined standard solutions. Diagnosis and therapy are not standard solutions, but the result of the comprehension of the specific problem thanks to the doctor's experience, preparation and knowledge. River basin reclamation and plans for urban growth need a good doctor, who knows how to recognise the problems.

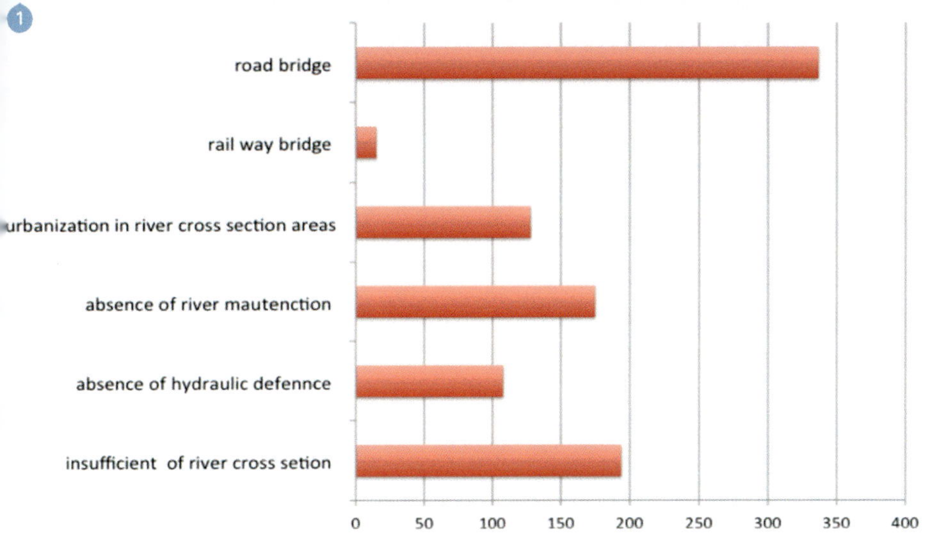

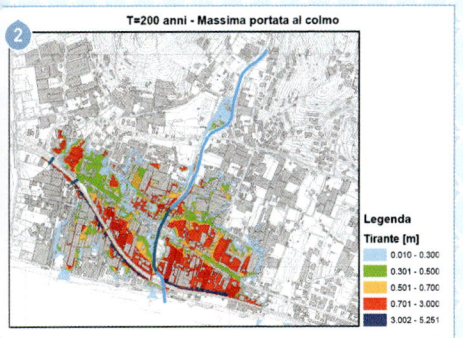
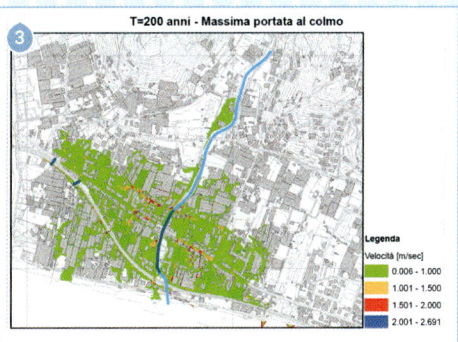

Img. 1 - Causes of the main "flood hazard": example of Sardinia Region (redrawn from P.A.I. report www.regione.sardegna.it). The figure shows how the main causes of hydraulic hazard are a result of the road bridge that most of time result under dimensioned respect to the design peak discharge.

Imgs. 2/3 - Hazard areas according to the F.W.D. The example of Verbone creek and the flooded area of Vallecrosia (Imperia, Italy)

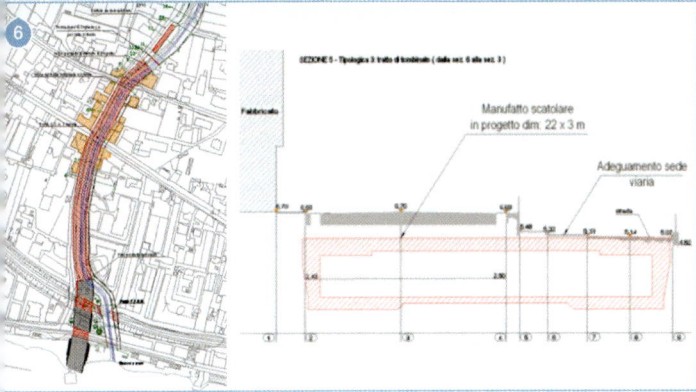

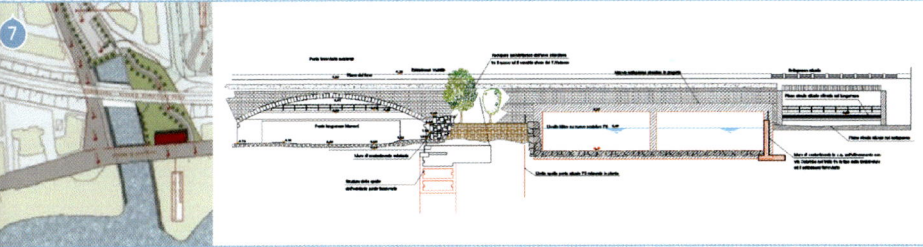

Img. 4 - The final reach of the Verbone creek crossing the town of Vallecrosia (sx) before reaching the Tyrrhenian Sea. The green line represent the part of river sections covered by a lead. (dx) The river bed at the beginning of the lead (green line).

Img. 5 - Structural defence works: Verbone creek example.
The design solution on a topographic map and the new cross section type.

Imgs. 6/7 - The Verbone creek mouth in the design configuration.
A new passage for the creek is created under the existing rail way embankment and a green pedestrian area is created on the previous river bed. The bottom part of the figure is presented the new cross section.

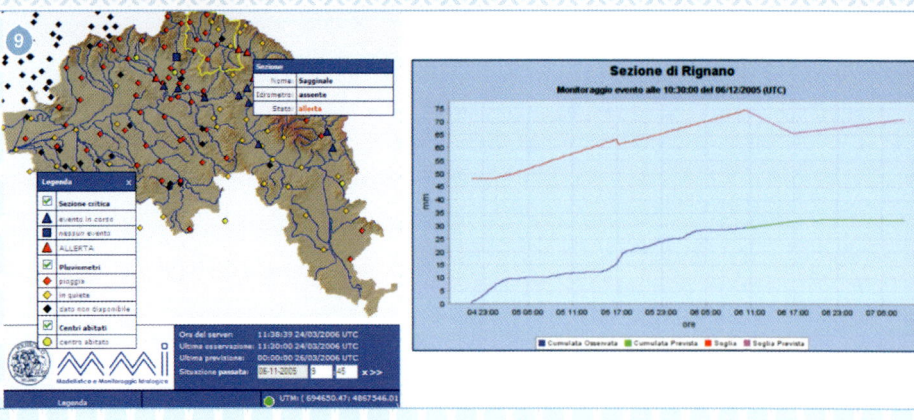

Img. 8 - River cross section restricted from building: the case study of the Quiliano creek (Savona Italy). From the upper left; the cross section reduced from buildings, the cross section enlargement design, the demolition of the house and the reconstruction of the historical bridge.
Img. 9 - Robust Flood Forecast system: the examples of rainfall warning thresholds for different river sections along the Arno River (Florence, Italy).
Img. 10 - Inundation of the northern area of Milan (Italy) September 2010.
Img. 11 - Flood Forecast system for the Seveso River in Milan: the example of flood hydrograph forecast coupling meteorological forecast and hydrological – hydraulic models. Any forecasted hydrograph (right side) is generated by rainfall forecasted 48 hours ahead (Seveso flood September 2010, Milan, Italy) The red line on the left side is the observed cumulative rainfall while the red line on the right is the inundation discharge of the river.

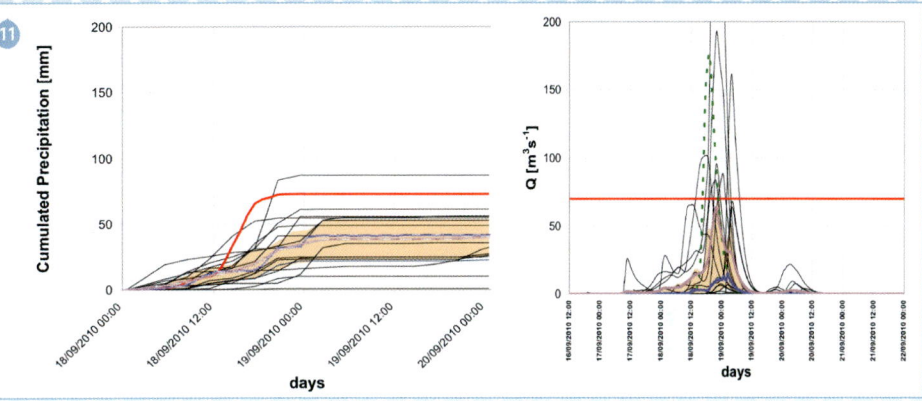

BUILDING

Common space:
Crossovers and hybridisations between architecture and water

70% of our body is made up of water and for nine months before coming into the world we grow and float in water. We therefore come from water, but as soon as we are born we forget this, all our activities and knowledge systems develop in a continuous confrontation with the earth on which we live and move around. For the whole of our life water remains a hostile, difficult environment, unavoidable in order to lead our lives but in which we feel much less at ease than on land. Without the use of water, it would not be possible to produce most of the elements and materials that we use for building the environments and cities in which we live. In some compounds, necessary for the construction of buildings, water is absolutely essential and is an integral part, such as for concrete. There are materials that when dry behave in a certain way and which, when wet, change nature, so to speak, and can be adapted to particular structures, taking on complex shapes. And, finally, others are moulded with water and then, when dried, take on their final shape, such as bricks. Finally, according to the World Health Organisation, one in eight people have no access to clean water, a somewhat alarming figure, almost equal to the 12% of global water resources consumed by the construction industry. We do even worse, consuming as much as 49%, when taking water to produce the energy needed to power our buildings.
If we look around, however, no trace remains of all the water we have used and which is necessary for the construction and functioning of these structures. Its isotropic and fluid nature means that, passing through our hands and our machinery, it evaporates, as if it were petrified without leaving any trace. Yet, if we think about it, water, rain, was one of the principal reasons that impelled man to search for a place for shelter. For the earliest humans it was initially a case of finding somewhere created by nature, able to offer shelter from the natural elements and, more generally, a place to take refuge from a hostile and uncontrollable natural environment. It is curious to note how these places were needed as protection from the rain but also, at the same time, as places in which to keep it and conserve it over time, for the use and survival of those living there. Paradoxically, the caves inhabited by the earliest humans brought together, in a single place, a hollow space in the rock, everything that was needed for life, shelter from the rain and, at the same time, a water container. They were therefore, if not in their shape and intentions, the best and most efficient water architecture that can be imagined. They provided shelter from the elements and the rain, which they absorbed and slowly released through the earth, conserving it and collecting it on the floor. Once man came out of the caves and built the first huts, the first examples of architecture, this natural coexistence was broken and we have lost

the close proximity between men and water. Thus, for a long time, not having the knowledge or tools to do otherwise, we concerned ourselves only with defending ourselves and supplying ourselves with water. In a kind of equilibrium between safety and the need to survive, these primitive constructions have become the expression of the measurement and of the distance between man and water. The measurement of our ability to store it and channel it, in substance the representation of our degree of dependence and, at the same time, our ability to control water. The stilt houses of our distant ancestors, apart from offering defence against wild animals, vertically measured our degree of possible distance from water, a sort of frontier, never a clear-cut borderline, but rather a place of comparison, capable of recording changes during the seasons, and of making advances with the development of technical and constructional knowledge. Gradually it has become less and less necessary to live so near to water and the more certain we have felt of being able to procure it without particular problems and risks, the more we have moved away from it. In other words we have placed an ever greater distance between ourselves and water, initially in a physical sense, and then, with the passage of time and advances in transport and storage systems, certainly also psychologically.

In between the earliest huts and our modern day architecture, this slow but inexorable detachment has been marked, however, by incredible and stupendous examples of architecture and infrastructure which were conceived from water and for water. Large constructions thus appeared in cities and landscapes in order to move and contain water, constructions which filled the distance and which, in a certain way, although separated, tied people and water together for a long time. Aqueducts, dams, tanks, canals, ditches, wells, spas, which represent, in a certain sense, man's emancipation from water and a clear declaration of his achieving the ability to control this precious liquid, created stupendous examples of water architecture, which give shape to and represent this frontier, achieving a very high aesthetic level. Then, after centuries of decline, with the advent of ever more sophisticated technologies, the development of hydraulic and engineering studies, and with interdisciplinary knowledge that exponentially increased the technical opportunities at every turn, these admirable structures, which had contributed to the design of cities and measured our landscapes, disappeared, buried under our streets, hidden and capillary inside the walls of our buildings (*Img. 1*). From a visible dimension, which transformed and sometimes directly gave rise to types of architecture, and which defined the character and structure of certain urban landscapes, we have passed into an invisible and hidden dimension. It is as if we passed from an evident volumetric dimension, that is to say the dimension of aqueducts, the impluvium and tanks, to a capillary one based on piping, valves and taps. Now nobody knows any more where the water they wash with comes from and cannot even think of following it back to its source. Now no man-made work, even if it is up-to-date or specialised, is able, in its relation with water, to express a typological development or any deep aesthetic renewal of architectural codes. Indeed, nowadays our cities are situated on the shores of lakes or stretch out along river banks but, apart from a few rare cases, they lack significant examples of water architecture, modern expressions of our present day relationship with water. Indeed, it is probable that our relationship has been, from a certain point onwards and up to the present, completely indifferent and extraneous to water. In other words, for a long time we have considered this resource to be unlimited and, with a few exceptions, certainly controllable and manageable. Starting from these considerations, and without making any particular efforts to store it and move it, we have forgotten it and we have lost interest in it and by doing so it has no longer been considered an element through which to define and reinvent architecture, its relationship with cities and with their inhabitants. Thus, our relationship with water, at first direct, and then mediated by architecture, has been impoverished, often wholly expressed and represented only through data and numbers, statistics and rules which regulate principles and quantities, but which struggle to produce visible and significant expressions of this complex system of rules or, indeed, of a new collective sentiment on this theme. Yet in the past, even the recent past, many architects have contended with this theme. They have often succeeded in building structures of high quality, each with his/her own poetics and, with a personal inflection of the theme, have created wonderful suspended structures, surrounded and enveloped by water. Frank Lloyd Wright's Fallingwater, Mies Van Der Rohe's Barcelona Pavilion, where water seemed to flow continually under the pavilion itself, Carlo Scarpa's Fondazione Querini Stampalia, or Louis I. Kahn's Parliament building in Dhaka are certainly examples in which water plays an important and essential role in the success of the building.

Beyond these, the hybridisation of the world of architecture with that of installation art has produced performative structures, almost always temporary, which have attempted to play a different role with water. As they are free from the constraints of traditional structures, performative and temporary structures have been able to play freely with spectacular effects and were the first to renew interest in a more intimate relationship between architecture and water. These temporary structures can only represent an intention, however, a passage, but they certainly cannot be the final outcome of a growing desire for appropriation of the ecological environmental and meaningful values that are carried by water. Numerous recent examples have forced the relationship with water in an ephemeral and playful direction, temporary and performative, defining the theme of coexistence between water and architecture in a direction more devoted to free time and to "wonder" than to a more realistic search for the coexistence and reciprocal need which can be established between buildings and water. This is the case, for example, of Diller and Scofidio's Blur; although the designers underline that the intention was not that of creating a cloud around the building to make it disappear, rather the cloud itself is the living space, they forget or do not notice that the living space they build is liveable only during the performance, only for a brief, magnificent and playful moment. None of these structures therefore manages to fully express the sense of this close relationship between buildings and water, nor that of the new demand for hybridisation between the two elements, which cannot be reduced merely to juxtaposition and to a game of cross-references, nor to a temporary effervescent theatrical performance, which belongs to a recent age but is now buried beneath the economic crisis and the crisis of meaning, which has altered the way we understand our relationship of necessity with nature and with the natural elements that surround us. The relationship between water and architecture is one that should not end up on the edge of the construction, but should innervate the whole building, which cannot be limited to a simple, though effective, juxtaposition. Architecture is undoubtedly a discipline that is slow to change and to represent the intentions, desires and visions of the future nurtured by the citizens that will have to live in its creations. It has often been dragged onto levels that are far removed from its true nature, design, with its reduced scale, installation art with its fragmentary temporality, have often produced positive and fruitful routes to hybridisation and renewal but, at the same time, have often distracted architecture from its more natural objective. Architecture can once again promote this new interest and contribute to shaping it. Now that we have become aware of the value of water as a finite resource, we are beginning to experiment again, in buildings and in urban settings; with new sensibility, architecture can once again play an important role as the natural setting for this regenerated desire for reconciliation (*Imgs. 2/3/4/5*). We are not talking about ephemeral flamboyance, but rather a renewed constructive intentionality which makes water the element through which to give shape to architecture. Collecting rain water, releasing it intelligently and distributing, storing and reusing it may restore the capacity of architecture to reinvent shapes and innovate typologies (*Imgs. 6/7/8/9/10/11*). The desire for reconciliation and the will to recover possession of a material that has provided architecture with enormous opportunity for expression is demonstrated by certain creations, and even more by publications and exhibitions, such as the exhibition "L'eau source d'architecture", an evocative title chosen by the architect and journalist Pascale Blin and by Francis Rambert, Director of the IFA/Cité de l'Architecture, for the photography exhibition at the Fondation Electricité de France in Toulouse (2000) which, organised into various themes and interpretations, presents projects created with the objective of demonstrating the extraordinary creative energy and power of suggestion exercised by water over the designers. Partly for fashion, partly out of duty, partly out of sincere interest and a change in sensibility, we now construct, more or less knowingly, buildings that collect the rain water that falls on their roofs, we store it in basements to use for watering our gardens and, in the best cases, we recover it and use it for flushing our lavatories.

The basements of our buildings are often filled with fire fighting tanks, lamination tanks of extraction wells and groundwater pumps. However, apart from rare cases, all this does not allow us to build a new, even aesthetic, dimension around this theme, a dimension that uses the form of architecture to fully express this strengthened and complex relationship between water and the buildings in which we live. In 1978, Renzo Piano and Richard Rogers presented the Beaubourg to the world. It was an urban animal which showed all its installation systems and equipment visibly on the outside. A little smugly the building showed with piping, ducts, vents and stairs how much of its real nature had, up to that point, been kept hidden. It is also true, however, that a basic premise for the success of a building is that of pursuing technologies and adopting techniques to "keep out" water, to separate wet spaces from dry ones. Perhaps we cannot expect too much, even though construction techniques have made enormous advances, as water remains a hostile element to the built world we live in, eroding, seeping and rusting. Despite all this, however, it is clear that there is new interest in the construction of opportunities for interaction between built space and water, between isotropic elements that contain and others that are, by nature, contained, giving rise to interesting experiments in coexistence and cohabitation. On the roofs of buildings, under factories, between the pillars of constructions, in courts and courtyards, water is slowly recapturing the functional and aesthetic space it had for a long time. Nowadays, however, advances in building techniques and the meeting of knowledge make it possible to create structures which can establish a new and more complex relationship with water. I do not mean just in terms of proximity but also in terms of hybridisations in which it is possible to mix spaces. Thus architecture, which is traditionally implanted in the ground and measures itself against the sky in which its shape is defined, can now also aspire to confront water in a more complex manner. Construction and control techniques give us the opportunity of building under and in water, of accommodating it inside buildings, of collecting it along surfaces and of outwardly showing its lymphatic system. Giving new meaning to collection, fire fighting and lamination tanks, highlighting the new nature of rain collection tanks on the roof, designing surfaces like a sponge able to capture water. Water in the structure and on the surface of our buildings could once again play a central role, both on an aesthetic and linguistic level, as well as on an energy and environmental level. Water could thus participate in the renewal of our cities, designing coatings for buildings capable of retaining water and of contributing intelligently and economically to the management of thermal exchange between the interior and exterior. Coatings capable of retaining water, ventilated façades, draining surfaces are capable of protecting the interior spaces of buildings and of mitigating the surrounding air by activating circulatory air flows. Horizontal and vertical veils of water, on the ground and on roofs and, above all, along façades, are capable of constructing a sophisticated ecosystem within cities, enabling discussion to be reopened also on the level of aesthetic and typological relations between architecture and water, starting from the level of technical efficiency achieved by our construction systems (*Img. 10*). In truth, certain examples have already been produced, such as the building known as SEWR, Solar Enclosure for Water Reuse. This is a façade system composed of modular elements in glass brick, glass blocks overlapping one another according to a precisely calculated outline and equipped with a rigid support for the collection of rainwater, flanked by a series of solar concentrators which capture and intensify the natural light inside the building. Mirroring and reflecting, dampening, crossing, are certainly systems and means of relating to water which are well known to architecture. As in certain examples mentioned above, many architects have contended with this theme with fascinating and exciting results, but perhaps, apart from particular attention to the work of Carlo Scarpa, almost nobody has succeeded in strongly unifying water, inside or on the surface of a building. We could, therefore, attempt to define certain themes and certain means of construction of new relationships between architecture and water, which could bring us closer to this precious and vital natural element in a more structural and less ephemeral way than has been achieved by recent contemporary architectural production.

A first approach could be that of "collecting" water. This operation, which already takes place in many forms, often only in order to conform with regulations, does not however produce any creative short circuits or any typological innovation, and the collection systems almost never have any effect on structures and on forms of architecture. In this sense it could be possible, as shown by certain early experimental cases, to outwardly express and highlight this desire and these regulatory guidelines. Water could be collected on roofs and façades, allowing our buildings to be transformed and highlighting this new sensibility. A second approach could be that of "containing" water inside our buildings. The yards of condominiums, terraces, patios and courtyards could once again contain water, collection tanks and impluvium. These new structures could renew the meaning of these often forgotten or underused places, reduced to bare spaces for parking bicycles and scooters. Water, as a bearer of micro-climatic benefits for the surrounding environment could succeed in renewing the collective nature of these places and of building around itself their rebirth as central places for the quality of the community living around them. A third possible approach is that of turning the surface of buildings "inside out" and making visible the capillary lymphatic system that supplies our buildings. Venous architecture carry on the outside on the surface, a little like in the drier parts of our body, the system of piping that feeds all the vital parts of buildings. A form of architecture that reveals its nature as that of a hydraulic machine that allows an external display of the network and the complexity of the system that feeds it. On façades and on roofs but also in stairwells and internally towards courtyards we could think of putting on view the water risers, collection or recovery tanks, the capillary structure of terminations as well as that of collection and channelling of rainwater.

A fourth approach could be that of "showing" water outside (*Imgs. 12/13/14*). There are numerous buildings that are created, for various reasons, to contain water inside. But some, more than others, have a strong tendency to interaction with citizens and with their users. Swimming-pools, spas and aquariums in particular build up, in different ways, an intimate relationship with their users (*Imgs. 15/16/17/18/19/20*). This relationship is, however, often only with those who take part or directly participate in the activities that take place within them. They are often organised according to rigid regulations, hidden from view, divided into closed boxes or, in any case, into containers that never reveal to the outside their intimate and complex relationship with the water they contain. For some time now, museums, residences and even places of worship, theatres and auditoriums, have attempted in different ways to open themselves up to the outside world, to the landscape, to the city, revealing their interior spaces, which previously were secret and could only be appreciated by those using them. These buildings have often sought a direct relationship with nature or with surrounding buildings and monuments, but in certain cases they have revealed themselves solely for the pleasure of opening themselves up to the city and unfreezing their secret mechanisms and the essence of their interior spaces.

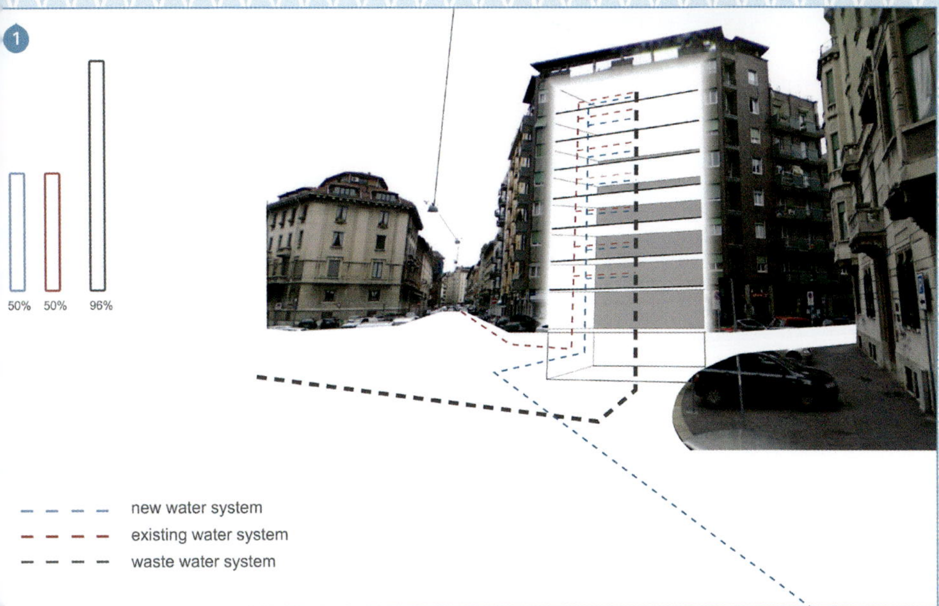

- - - new water system
- - - existing water system
- - - waste water system

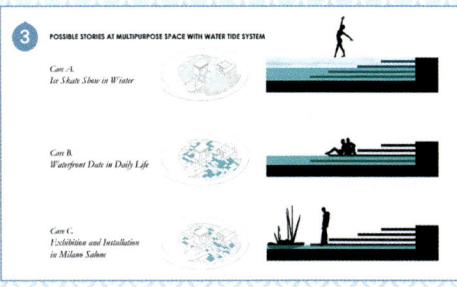

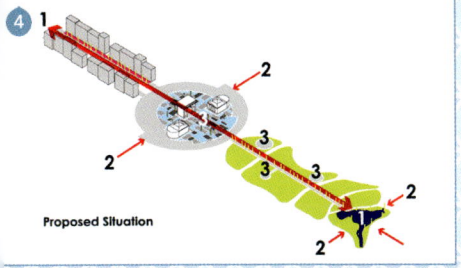

Proposed Situation

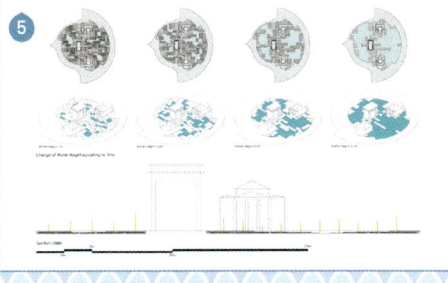

Img. 1 - **System housing zone, from Water City by Karl Maisinger, 2010.**
Imgs. 2/3/4/5 - **Image by Hideaki Nishimura from "Triadic water concerto" - Final Master Project 2011.**

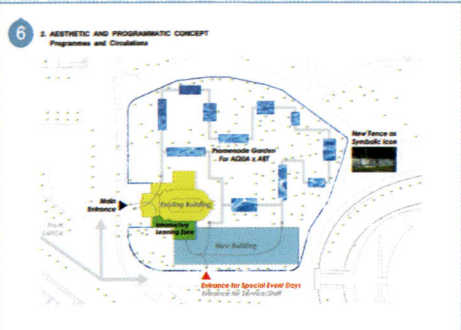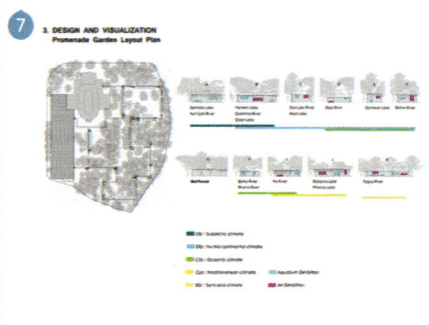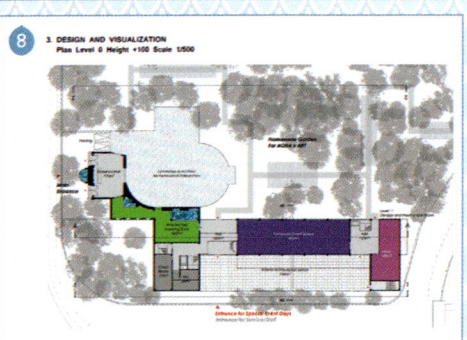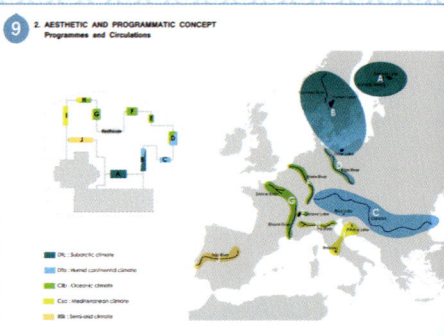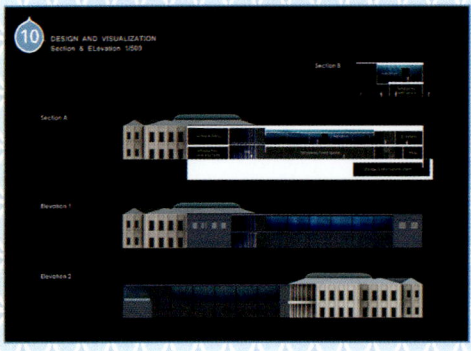

Imgs. 6/7/8/9/10/11 - Image by Hideaki Nishimura from "Triadic water concerto" - Final Master Project 2011.
Imgs. 12/13/14/15/16/17 - Images by Jin Young Kim from "Diving Pool" - Workshop: Water as Urban Type, 2011

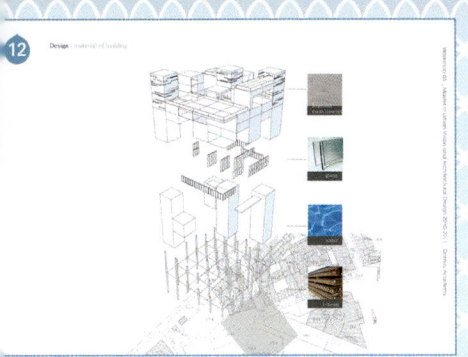
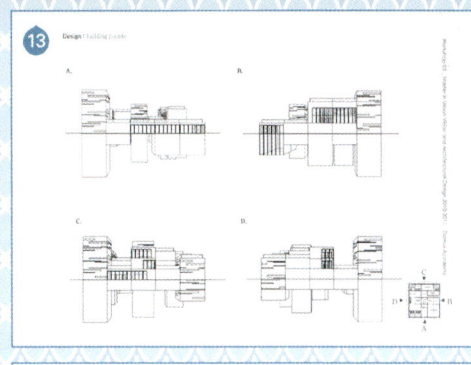
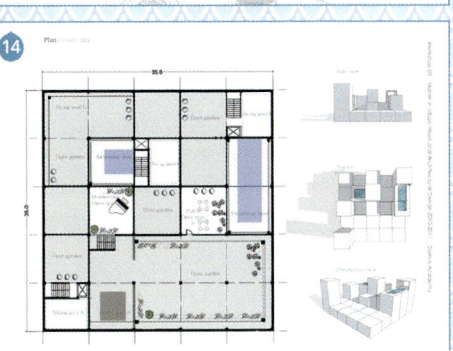
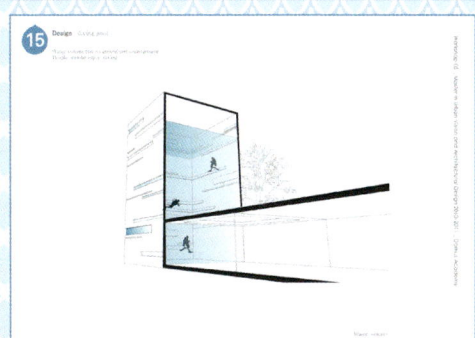
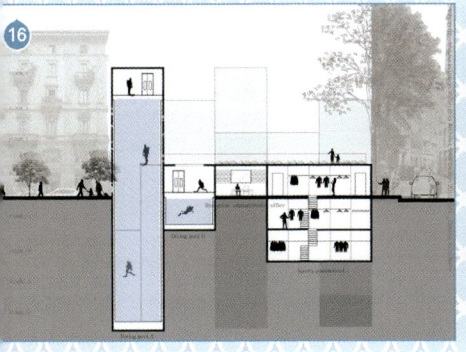

G. BARRECA

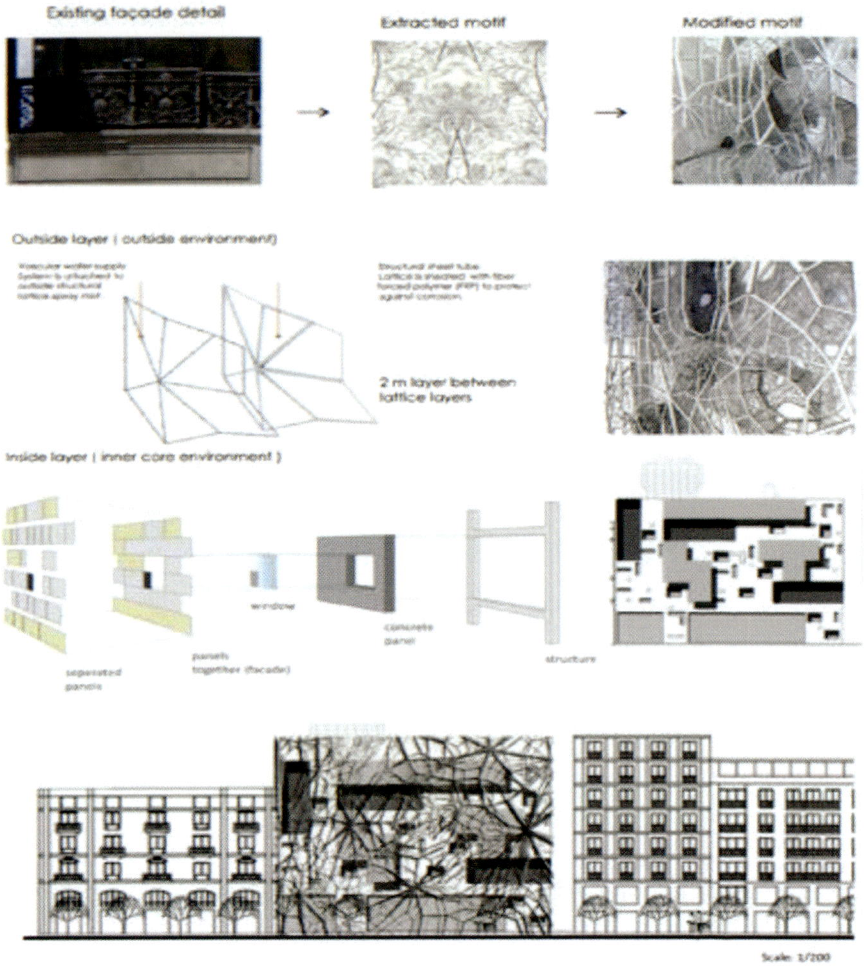

Img. 18 - Skin concept. Project: Diving Pool, by Jin Young Kim - Workshop: Water as Urban Type, 2011.
Img. 19 - Sustenible skin. Project: Diving Pool, by Charbel Attieh - Workshop: Water as Urban Type, 2011.
Img. 20 - Concept design. Project: Diving Pool, by Charbel Attieh - Workshop: Water as Urban Type, 2011.

19

Sustainable approach

Winter time

Summer time

Sustainable skin

Thermal diagram

Luminosity diagram

3d Skin concept

3d Views

20

Section DD
scale 1/200
10.00 am 30 May 2011

Section DD
16.00 pm 30 May 2011

Section GG
scale 1/200

Section FF
scale 1/200

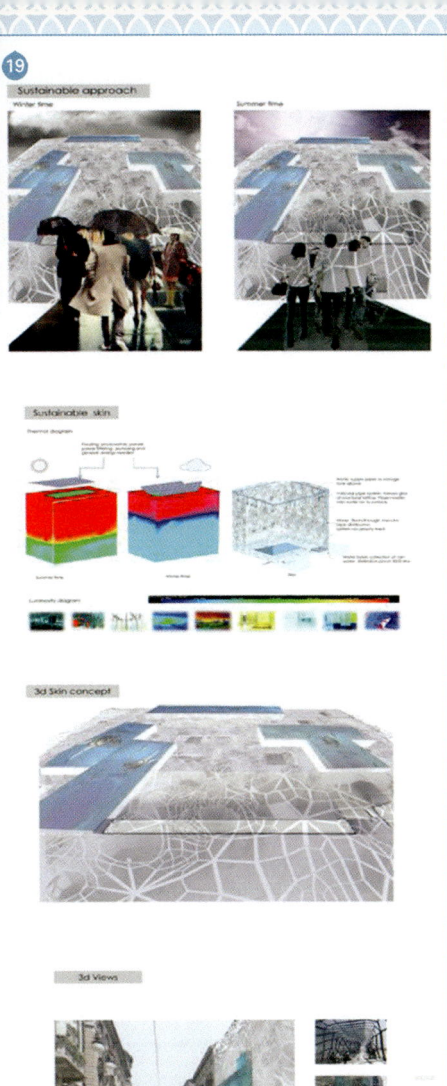

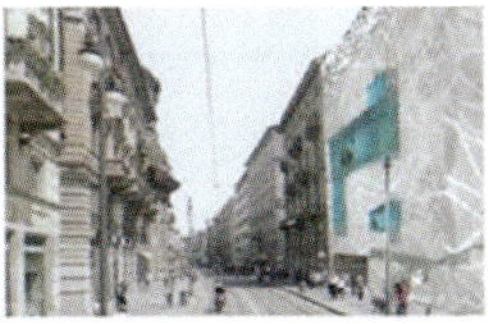

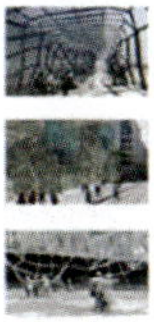

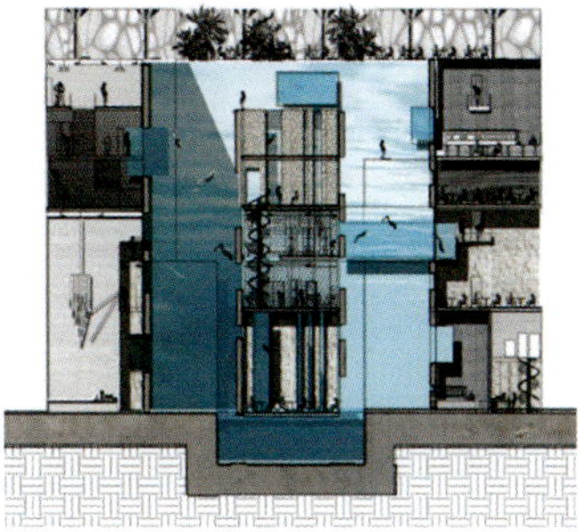

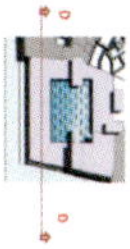

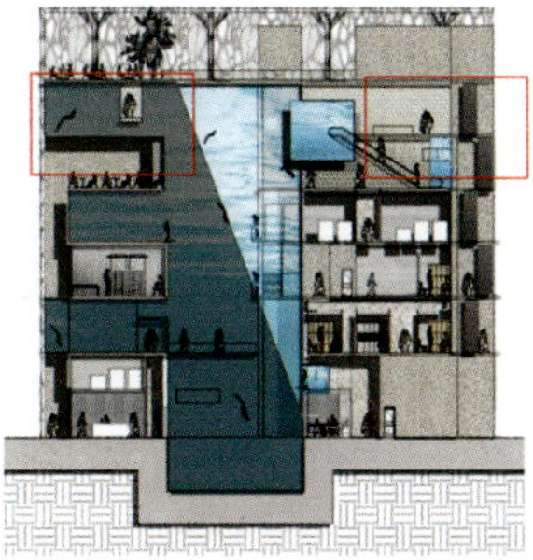

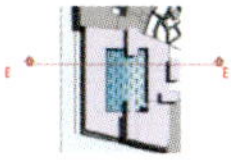

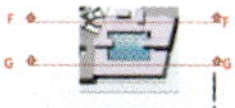

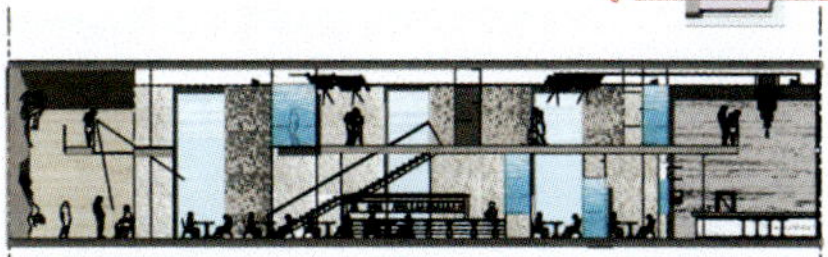

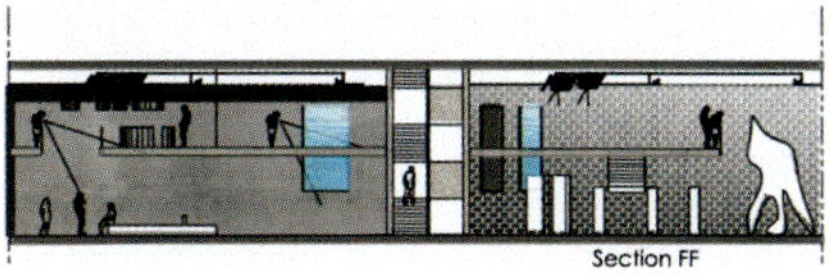

Martesana Canal:
New ways of living along the water.
Water as architecture

1. The Martesana canal

It has been over five centuries since the Duke of Milan, Francesco Sforza, began the excavation of the Martesana canal. Since then, the channel has represented, gradually over the centuries, for the municipalities that crossed or lapped, but also for the adjacent villages, an artery of primary economic importance. The freight transportation, irrigation of the fields and the energy production for the mills have been a driving force for the development and the social growth of the whole basin. However, the Martesana was not only an economic support but also a place for the wealthy Milanese, their leisure and summer holidays: along its banks patrician villas of artistic and historical value were built and still exist.

More recently, the channel has lost its original function, but still conserves the strong historical and social value, not only for the communities most directly affected, but also for the long swathes of land contiguous to the banks that consists of over 40 municipalities which, over the centuries, have traded and had cultural exchanges, thanks to the presence of the new connection system with the closest villages and with Milan, where the Naviglio ends its run. Now that the Martesana no longer serves for which it was built, still retains something of its charm and its original interest.

Martesana Canal, which is part of the northern system of Milan Navigli, runs from the Adda River, in the vicinity of Trezzo sull'Adda, to Milan. Approximately 38 kilometres long, with a substantial section covered over or infilled, Martesana defines a linear system and a rich and complex environmental and cultural identity just along its path, which testifies the ever-existed relation among water, land and man. Heterogeneous architectures, related to different historical periods and to diverse purposes, are scattered along the river path and prove the impact of the water on the territory and on the human activities.

The farmhouses are the traces of the rural identity of the valley, of its agricultural production enriched by the canal water. Villas are the memory left from the ancient nobility, who appreciated the suggestive landscape beauty; the churches belong to the small rural communities; the old production sites, which exploited the energy of water, describe the first industrialization process of Lombardy. Today, the presence of Naviglio has no impact on the territorial growth: Martesana is not anymore conceived as a resource and the urbanization process simply follows its own rules. A new path of investigation is needed: the exploration of the site, its architecture and its natural aspects.

2. Urban, suburban and rural

Following the canal basin from the end to its beginning, the essence of the canal starting from Milano to its source, Trezzo D' Adda, shows the relationship between the city an its countryside. The first part of the Martesana is completely urban and insisting in the city central areas. The banks of the canal are almost entirely built, the front of multi storey buildings, court houses and small cottages, creates a discontinuous and a little messy front, interrupted only occasionally by secondary channels and small plots of land. Its banks randomly open onto squares, small parks and open areas left in between constructions. At the edge of the city, when the built environment dissolves into a diffused system, the channel becomes the connection between small villages and the town. For a long stretch then, the channel has no front, and just few crossings between long frames of cultivated nature. Water, emptied of its economic and commercial significance, becomes the link from city to countryside, and crosses a piece of scenery hardly explored.

A long bicycle path only follows the linear system of the Martesana canal, currently an agglomerate of three completely different landscapes, the canal and its crossings. The subway that at one moment arises on the surface, at the boundary between the city and its periphery, serves half of its course. The main road follows part of its run and right after the city detaches from the banks abandoning the waterway to cross the agricultural lands.

3. A linear system and its fragmented surroudings

After a deep and detailed investigation of the urban structure of the banks the students traced an overview on the different typologies that are insisting on the two sides of the canal. The analysis considered the urban structure crossed by the Martesana canal, starting from the most urban one, the Milanese part, all along its bed: Vimodrone, Cassina dé Pecchi, Gorgonzola, Bellinzago, Inzago and Trezzo d' Adda. The survey posed its attention to the historical, scattered stratification of buildings and public spaces and underlined its critical points. Students then selected a specific area and completed an existing void with a strategical intervention. The work offered the opportunity for reinventing the relation between water and human settlement, by experiencing new ways of living along the water. Starting from a proper analysis aiming to clarify the multiple layers which characterize the linear strip of land along the water way, the focus moved on the building typologies that could be adopted to structure the site, and to create a quality habitat that benefited from the passage of the water channel. Apart from defining the proper solution in terms of concept, typology, spatial layout and details, the design of the ground level required a special attention, in order to connect building and water, the two entities that survive close one to each other, but in fact are separate and respectively indifferent. The relationship between the project and the water became seminal and the proposed solution tried to solve the missing link between the built environment and the canal. Water, in this case, was considered not only as a resource, in terms of environmental quality, but also as an integrated part of the design. The thesis explored the possibilities to re-invent the relationship between the water and the built environment by considering the full section of the canal, underlining the relationship between the buildings, the river bank, the existing public spaces and the street; the conditions of the residential areas, suggesting a new conception of urban villa, taking into account the new demand of housing close to a natural environment and the existing potential of the site re-considering the possibility to create self-sustainable housing systems. The projects entirely used the given resources, using water as possible architectural element.

4. Water building

The project "Green is good, blue is better" takes advantage of a left over suburban area and proposes a series of different typological interventions, after exploring new ways of living along the water. The existing built environment, as analyzed, is fragmented and doesn't take into account the existence of the river. The series of mid, high-rise apartment blocks and the single unit dwellings share little in common with the idea of creating a system that involves water into the construction. On the contrary, the proposal, inserts into a newly created water system, obtained deviating its course, innovative ways of building with water. The result is a catalogue of small interventions where a cantilevered house incorporates a swimming pool, a stilt house uses a system of water purification and water farming, and finally, an edge house includes a system of rainwater harvesting. A series of small gardens and water channels includes innovative ways of dealing with water, and not only brings back the forgotten relationship but also uses it as architectural element, influencing the design as well as the living condition of its future inhabitants.

The project "cultivation housing" takes a completely different path. The selected site insists on the border of the city of Milano, where the river Lambro meets the Martesana canal. The now completely abandoned area is almost an island, secluded in between two waterways and the main suburban road. The proposal includes the creation of a completely new system of water connections that crosses the land with a regular matrix of canals in which a new residential area is imagined. The project takes its inspiration from the existing small and informal vegetables gardens that were built, across the years, along the Martesana by the local community, and enhances its potentials. The project multiplies the waterfronts, substitutes roads with waterways, and creates private and public gardens. Each residential unit is provided with a small, private water farm, and the public space allow a public experience of the farming activities. A temporary open market can be used by the inhabitants to sell products and creates a pleasant natural environment. The project, although being conscious of the difficulties risen by the innovative spirit of the intervention, revivals a forgotten part of the city and the river, enhancing its natural aspects to pure resources of wellbeing and nurturing a new residential environment.

Both proposals are a demonstration of how architecture can deal with water in a new friendly and collaborative way, even in contemporary times. The channel, having lost its original economical and connective significance becomes a source of inspiration for new ways of living along the water.

Img. 1 - **Life style around Martesana, vegetable garden. Image by Jin Young Kim from "Coultivation housing" - Final Master Project 2011.**
Img. 2 - **Spatial layouts, this layers shows that how possibility of layout and how is connected with water. Duble house separated, duble house, triple house, Latest layout suggest that more various and rich farming environment. Image by Jin Young Kim from "Coultivation housing" - Final Master Project 2011.**

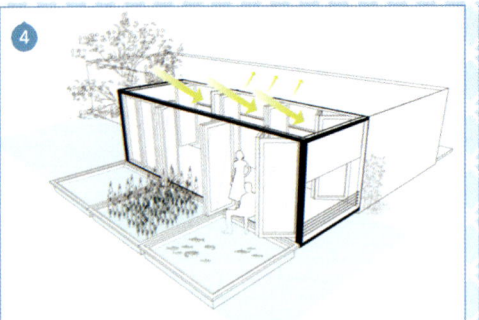
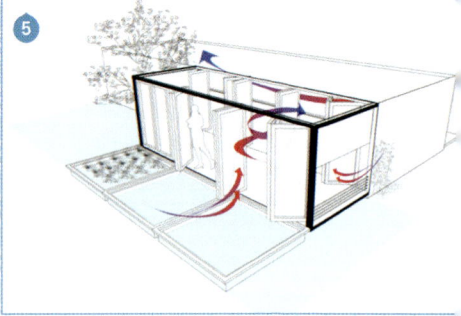

Img. 3 - **Section of housing** .
Image by Jin Young Kim from "Coultivation housing" - Final Master Project 2011.
Img. 4 - **Lightening diagram, natural lightening** .
Image by Jin Young Kim from "Coultivation housing" - Final Master Project 2011.
Img. 5 - **Ventilation diagram, natural ventilation** .
Image by Jin Young Kim from "Coultivation housing" - Final Master Project 2011.
Img. 6 - **Elements of house.**
Image by Jin Young Kim. Project title: "Coultivation housing" - Final Master Project 2011.
Img. 7 - **Public water farming.**
Image by Jin Young Kim. Project title: "Coultivation housing" - Final Master Project 2011.

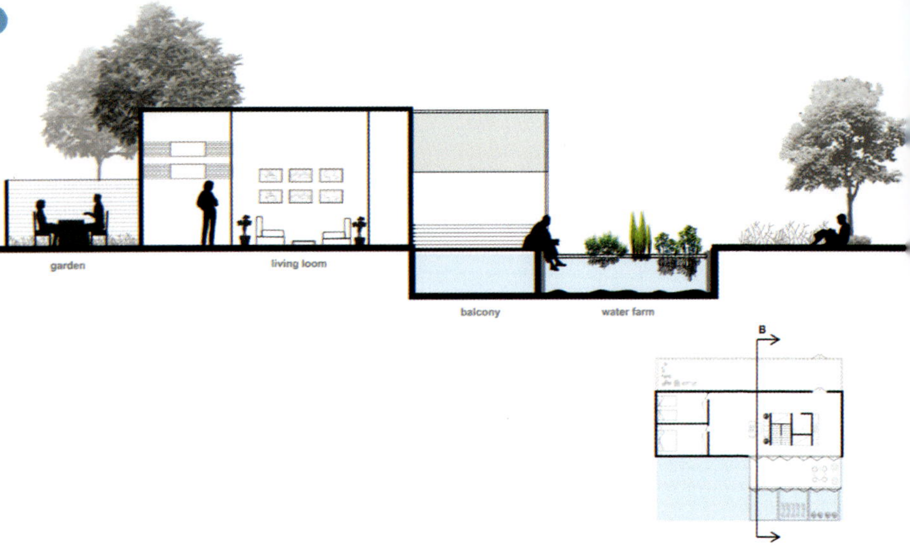

BUILDING

⑥

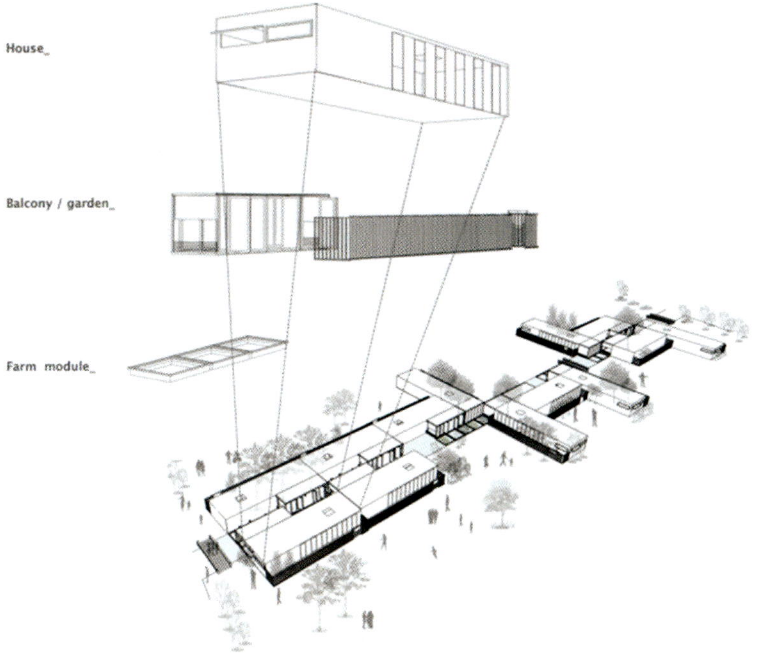

House_

Balcony / garden_

Farm module_

⑦

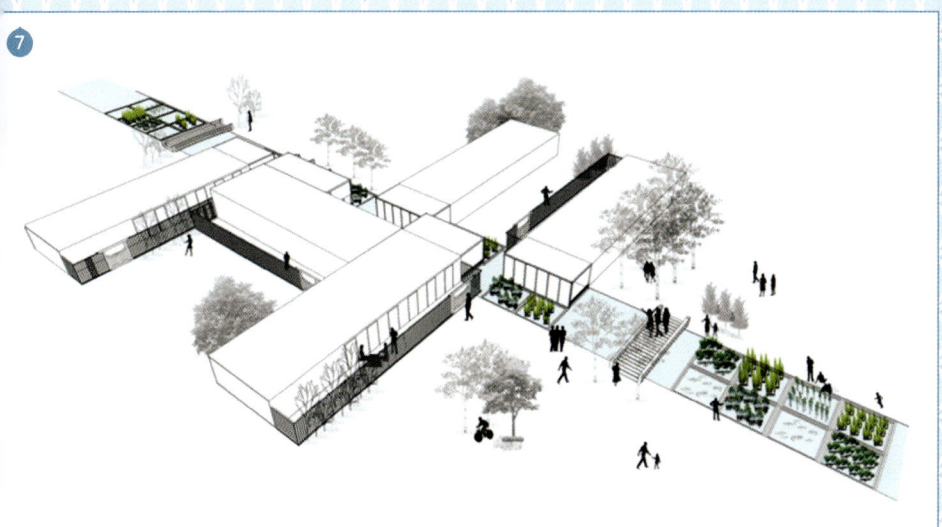

BIBLIOGRAPHY

Between Policies and Urban Perception (p. 36)

- Barreca, Gianandrea. Interview with Sean Yam. Recorded personal interview. Milano, October 2, 2011. Barreca, Gianandrea. Interview with Sean Yam. Recorded personal interview. Milano, October 2, 2011."Ipotesi (realistiche) per riportare l'acqua a Milano." Linkiesta (Milano). June 25, 2011. http://www.linkiesta.it/ipotesi-realistiche-riportare-l-acqua-milano. Accessed: June 30, 2011.
- Boeri, Stefano. biomilano. Mantua, Italy: Corraini Edizioni, 2011.
- Branzi, Andrea. "For a New Athens Charta." Milano: Studiobranzi, 2010.
- Cassia, Macchi, et al. X Milano. Milano: Hoepli, 2004.
- Clément, Gilles. Manifesto for the Third Landscape. Milano: Quodlibet, 2005.
- Comune di Milano e Camera di commercio Milano. Io amo Milano, 2006.
- Covic, Ivo. Interview with Sean Yam. Recorded personal interview. Milano, September 21, 2011.
- Dreiseitl, Herbert, and Grau, Dieter. New Waterscapes: Planning, Building and
- Designing with Water. Berlin: Birkhauser, 2005.
- Fabian, Lorenzo, and Viganò, Paola. Eds. Extreme City: Climate Change and the Transformation of the Waterscape. Venezia: IUAV di Venezia, 2010.
- Foot, John. Milan Since the Miracle. Oxford: Berg Publishers, 2001.
- Ghidoni, Matteo. Interview with Sean Yam. Recorded personal interview. Milano, September 19, 2011.
- Hales, Mike.; King, Samanth.; Pena, Andres Mendoza. The Urban Elite: The A.T.
- Kearney Global Cities Index 2010. Chicago: A.T. Kearney Inc., 2010.
- Lembi, Pietro. Interview with Sean Yam. Recorded personal interview. Milano, September 7, 2011.
- Leto, Alessandro. Interview with Sean Yam. Recorded personal interview. Lugano, Switzerland, September 20, 2011.
- Mancini, Marco. Interview with Sean Yam. Recorded personal interview. Milano, September 12, 2011.
- Marinetti, F.T. "The Founding and Manifesto of Futurism."
- (http://www.italianfuturism.org/manifestos/foundingmanifesto/Futurist Manifesto) from Apollonio, Umbro, Ed. Documents of 20th Century Art: Futurist Manifestos. Brain, Robert, R.W. Flint, J.C. Higgitt, and Caroline Tisdall, trans. New York: Viking Press, 1973. 19-24. (First published in French, Le Figaro, Paris, 1909).
- Metrogramma. Piano di Governo del Territorio. Milano: Comune di Milano, 2005, in The Plan, #47 (December 2010/ January 2011), 38-93.
- Pugliese, Raffaele, and Lucchini, Marco. Milano: citta' d'acqua. Firenze: Alinea, 2009. 2010. The Waterworks Basics. Milano. Metropolitana Milanese SpA.
- http://www.metropolitanamilanese.it/pub/page/en/MM/come_funziona_acquedotto. Accessed: September 30, 2011.
- White, Iain. Water and the City: Risk, Resilience and Planning for a Sustainable Future.
- London: Taylor and Francis, 2010.
- Vigano', Paola. Interview with Sean Yam. Recorded personal interview. Milano, September 12, 2011.
- Yam, Sean Frederic. Still Waters Run Deep: A Manifesto for the Water Systems

of the Milanese Metropolis [Masters Thesis]. Milano: MUVAD, Department of Urban and Landscape Design, Domus Academy, 2011.

Open spaces and the water cycle in the scattered urbanization of piedmont Lombardy (p. 98)

- Pierre Bélanger, "Landscape as Infrastructure", Landscape Journal, Vol. 28, n. 1, 79-95, 2009.
- Stefano Boeri, Arturo Lanzani e Edoardo Marini, Il territorio che cambia, Ambienti, paesaggi e immagini della regione Milanese, Abitare Segesta, Milano, 1993.
- Michel Desvigne, Intermediate natures, Birkhäuser, Basel, 2009.
- Diap-Politecnico di Milano e Provincia di Milano, La città di città. -Un progetto strategico per la regione urbana milanese, 2006.
- Arturo Lanzani e Gabriele Pasqui, L'Italia al futuro, Città e paesaggi, economie e società, Arturo Lanzani, Alessandro Alì, Daniela Gambino, Antonio Longo, Anna Moro, Christian Novak, Federico Zanfi, Quando l'autostrada non basta. Infrastrutture, paesaggio e urbanistica nel territorio
pedemontano, Macerata, Quodlibet, 2013.
- Franco Angeli, Milano, 2011.
- Mohsen Mostafavi (editor), Ecological Urbanism, Harvard University Graduate school of design/Lars Muller, Harvard/Baden, 2010.
- Erich R. Trevisiol, Ciclo delle acque e ambiente costruito, Il sole 24 ore, Milano, 2002.
- Kazys Varnelis, The infrastructural city: Networked ecologies in Los Angeles, Actar, Barcelona, 2008.
- Charles Waldheim (editor), The landscape urbanism reader, Princeton Architectural Press, New York, 2006.
- Federico Zanfi e Daniela Gambino, Le radure della Brianza centrale. Un progetto per gli ultimi spazi aperti della città diffusa, in Lanzani et al., 2013, cit. pp. 128-155.spazi aperti della città diffusa, in Lanzani et al., 2013, cit. pp. 128-155.

Urban growth in the river valley (p. 122)

- ACQWA project (Assessing Climate Impacts on the Quantity and quality of WAter), EC-WP7 www.acqwa.ch, 2013.
- Ceppi, A., Ravazzani, G., Rabuffetti, D., Mancini, M. (2010), Evaluating the uncertainty of hydrological model simulations coupled with meteorological forecasts at different spatial scales. Procedia - Social and Behavioral Sciences, Volume 2, Issue 6, 2010, Pages 7631-7632.
- Dovera, D., M. Mancini, M. Salis, Linee Guida per l'attività di individuazione e perimetrazione delle aree a rischio idraulico e geomorfologico e delle relative misure di salvaguardia [Guidelines for identification and delimitation of hydraulic and geomorphological risk areas and of the relevant safeguarding measures] (L 267/98), ed. Regione SARDEGNA, 2000.
- Hall J. W., and E. C. Penning-Rowsell, Setting the scene for the flood risk management, in Flood risk and management, Blackwell Publishing, Ltd, 2011.
Luna B. Leopold, M. Gordon Wolman,

John P. Miller. Fluvial processes in geomorphology. New York: Dover Publications. ISBN 0-486-68588-8, 1995.
MAIDMENT, D. R., Handbook of Hydrology, ed. D.R. Maidment, McGraw-Hill INC., isbn 0-07-039732-5, 1993.
- Munich Reinsurance Company (Munich Re): Topics Geo natural catastrophes 2010: analyses, assessments, positions, Munich Re, Mu nchen, Germany, 52 pp., 2011.
Penning-Rowsell, E. C. Coping with extreme flood, warnings, impacts and responses, the extreme of the extreme: extraordinary floods, International association of Hydrologic Sciences, v. 271, pp.379-383, 2002.
- Mancini, M., F. Valsecchi , Un sistema informativo ai fini di protezione civile per l'analisi del rischio di esondazione indotto dai ponti stradali: il caso di studio della Provincia di Lecco [An information system for the purposes of civil protection to anyalse flood risks caused by road bridges: the case study of the Province of Lecco], Ambiente e Territorio, 2007.
- FEMA, Federal Emergency Management Agency, 2002. Guidelines and specifications for flood hazard mapping partners. FEMA Publications.2002.
- Rabuffetti, D., Ravazzani, G., Corbari, C., Mancini, M., Verification of operational Quantitative Discharge Forecast (QDF) for a regional warning system – the AMPHORE case studies in the upper Po River. Nat. Hazard Earth Sys. 8, 161-173, 2008.
- Ravazzani, G., Mancini, M., Giudici, I., Amadio, P., Effects of soil moisture parameterization on a real- time flood forecasting system based on rainfall thresholds. In: Quantification and Reduction of Predictive Uncertainty for Sustainable Water Resources Management (Proceedings of Symposium HS2004 at IUGG2007, Perugia, July 2007), IAHS Publ. 313, 407-416., 2007.
- Ravazzani G, Mancini M, Meroni C: Design hydrograph and routing scheme for flood mapping in a dense urban area. Urban Water Journal 6(3), 221-231, doi: 10.1080/15730620902781434, 2009.
- Ravazzani.G P. Gianoli, S. Meucci, M. Mancini, Indirect estimation of design flood in urbanized river basins using a distributed hydrological model, J Hydrologic Engineering, ASCE doi 10.1061/(ASCE)HE.1943-5584.0000764, 2013.

Published by
**LISt Lab Laboratorio
Internazionale Editoriale**
Italy - Via Esterle, 26
38100, Trento
Italy - Spain - Netherlands
info@listlab.eu
www.listlab.eu

Producted by
GreenTrenDesign Factory
Piazza Manifattura, 1
38068 Rovereto (TN) - ITALY
T: +39 0464 443427
info@greentrendesign.it

Curated by
**Gianandrea Barreca,
Domus Academy**

Translations
Louise Judge

Editorial Director
Pino Scaglione

Editorial Assistant
Gioia Marana

Graphic design (artdir.)
Massimiliano Scaglione,
with collaboration of
Alberto Frecina

ISBN **9788895623528**

**Printed and bound in European Union,
August 2014**

**all rights reserved
© of the edition, LISt
© of the texts, the authors
© of the images, the authors**

Promotion and Ditribution
**ITALY - Messaggerie Libri, Spa, Milano
SPAIN & PORTUGAL - Inédit
INTERNATIONAL - Actar D, New York**

LISt Lab is an editorial workshop, based in Europe, that works on contemporaneity. LISt Lab not only publishes, but also researches, proposes, promotes, produces, creates networks.

GreenTrenDesign Factory, member of Progetto Manifattura, is a multiplatform structure, that provides advanced design services. In the balance between sustainability and quality, craftsmanship and digital experimentation, the company operates in partnership with LISt Lab.

LISt's Scientific Board
Eve Blau (Harvard GSD), Pepe Barbieri (Università di Chieti), Eva Castro (Architectural Association, London), Maurizio Carta (Università di Palermo), Alberto Clementi (Università di Chieti), Alberto Cecchetto (Università di Venezia), Stefano De Martino (Università di Innsbruck), Corrado Diamantini (Università di Trento), Antonio De Rossi (Università di Torino), Franco Farinelli (Università di Bologna), Carlo Gasparrini (Università di Napoli), Manuel Gausa (Università di Genova), Giovanni Maciocco (Università di Sassari/Alghero), Antonio Paris (Uniroma, Roma La Sapienza), Vanni Pasca (Emeritus), Josè Luis Esteban Penelas (Università di Madrid), Mosè Ricci (Università di Genova), Roger Riewe (Università di Graz), Pino Scaglione (Università di Trento).

LISt Lab is a green company committed to respect the environment. Paper, ink, glues and all processings come from short supply chains and aim at limiting pollution. The print run of books and magazines is based on consumption patterns, thus preventing waste of paper and surpluses. LISt Lab aims at the responsibility of the authors and markets, towards the knowledge of a new publishing culture based on an intelligent resource management.